CRICUT PROJECT IDEAS

VOL. 2

HUNDREDS OF FABULOUS PROJECTS FOR YOUR
EVENTS AND FOR YOUR HOME

Made with love

by

Sienna

Tally

TABLE OF CONTENTS

Introduction

Thank you for purchasing the sequel to "Cricut Projects ideas vol. 1 ": "Cricut Projects vol. 2".
In this brand new guide, I, Sienna Tally, will show you more wonderful and colorful projects to do with your cricut machines. We'll continue to uncover various ideas based on the type of material used, but in part 2 I'll guide you to discover new ideas for events that every year require a great creative effort such as Halloween, Valentine's Day and Easter.

Translated with www.DeepL.com/Translator (free version) In the past, choosing a design could cause epic proportional migraines, but it's a different story now. The famous Cricut computer is responsible for cutting paper, vinyl, and cloth based on a specific pattern or design. The print or template can be produced or modified using a Cricut Design Studio program.
When you purchase your Cricut machine, you will be excited to get started. Search the online Cricut library for ideas on creating cool projects that will make your environment more enjoyable and a project that you can use to give others joy in their life, such as cards and wooden signs.
The craftier you are, the more fun this new machine that you have purchased will provide you. If you are ready to get crafting, then I suggest you take this book and the other manual that came with your Cricut and begin learning all the tools and tips

that I have included. This will help bring you one step closer to being a master crafter when using your Cricut.

You can create your paper, allow it to dried up completely, then media with your iron (no steam).

You can use your paper to produce simple type scrapbooks or cards and one of your kind embellishments. Items nobody else has or will understand how to copy regardless of how difficult they try. This can allow your designs to create original scrapbooks using a range of colors and textures that can't be duplicated.

The chipboard shouldn't be worn, or you will damage the blades. You need to keep monitor of the edge's sharpness so that you can continuously enjoy an alternative if required.

Heavier grade of cardstock could cause blades to flat faster. This means you will have the chance to purchase thinner, more affordable paper or cardstock.

This book levels up your game up in the crafting business. The expert qualities that you shall learn from this book will take you on a journey of setting up your own business by making and selling wonderful Cricut designs. Now it is up to you to decide whether you want to step up your level to become a successful crafter of all time or you just want to stick to the basics. Expert level is the real thing in the crafting game. A lengthy illustrative five expert level projects are enough to equip you with every sort of powerful skill to enable you in the masters of Cricut designs In this detailed guide, you'll discover the top project Ideas to skyrocket with your Cricut Projects in 2021.

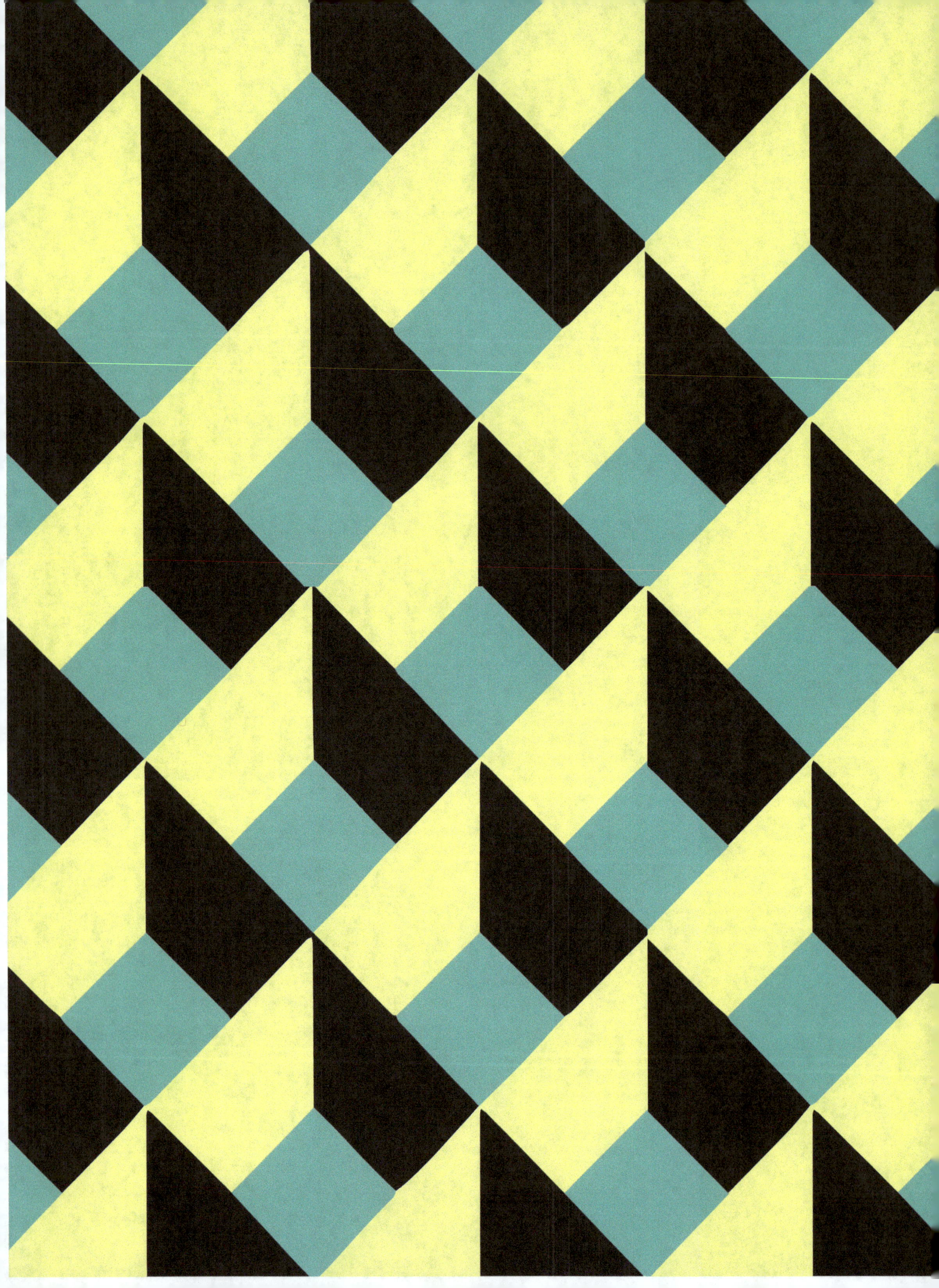

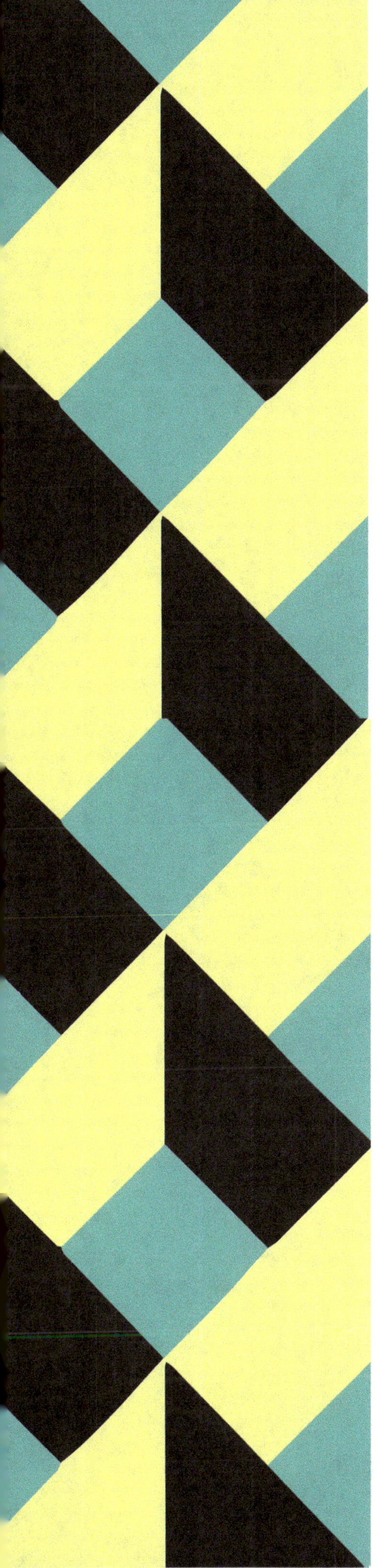

Chapter 1
Leather

PAPER FERENS RESIN SERVING TRAY DIY

MATERIALS NEEDED

Bamboo service tray
High-gloss Envirotex Lite resin
Green shade paper
Ultra seal
Cricut Explore Air 2 machine
White paint
Resin instruction manual handles, cups and sticks

DIRECTION

Start with paint inside the tray.
Cut the leafy ferns into three colors of green paper during drying on the tray.
Good ferns and fronds should be available to fill the tray.
Then make straight lines on the blades with a straight edge and cutter.
It fits snugly on the tray's edges.
Once cut and fit on the tray, cover with the Ultra Seal the bottom of the tray, then place the leaves above and cover the top with an additional Ultra-Seal. It can slightly bubble up. Don't panic. Completely let it dry.

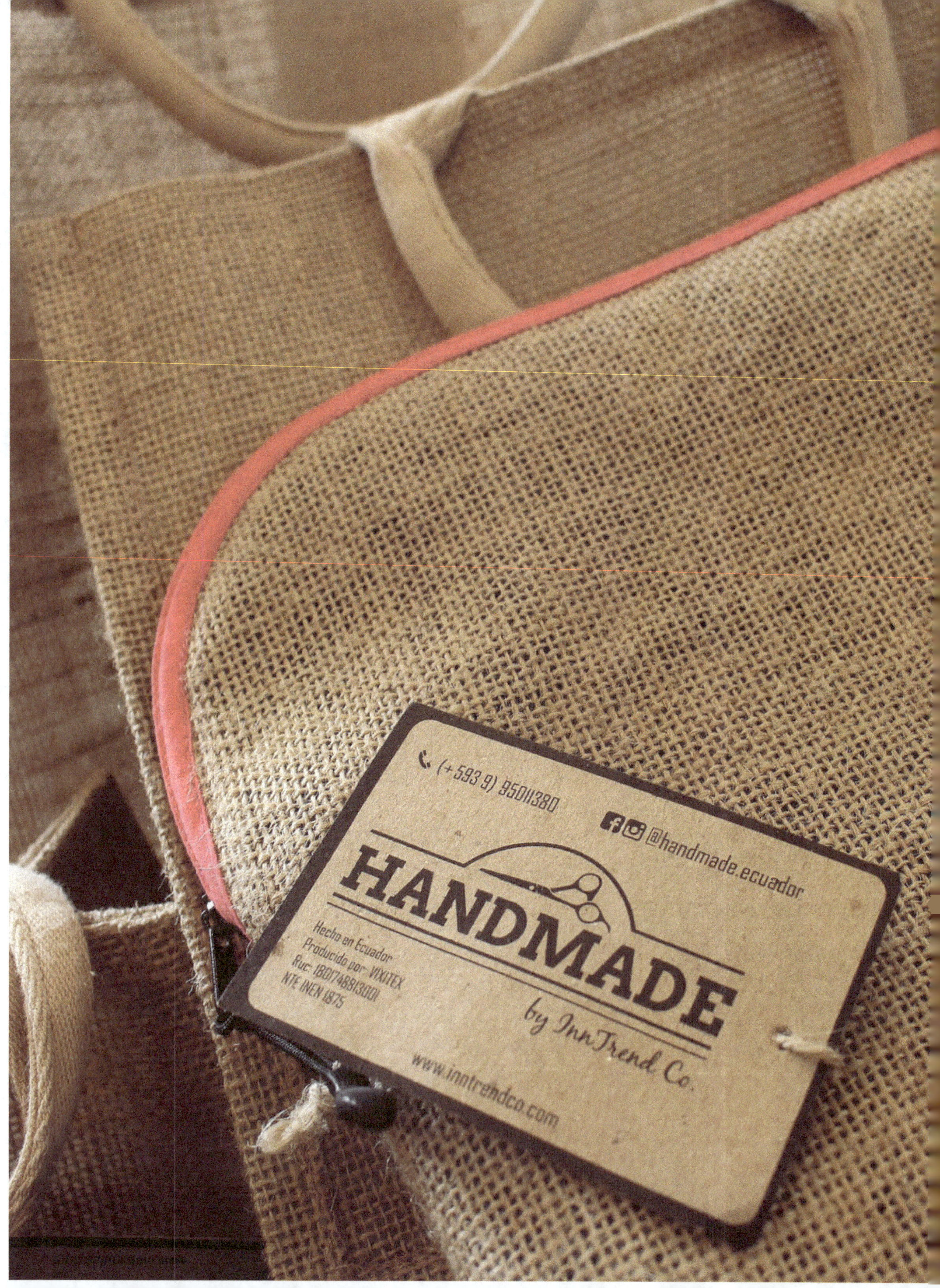
(+593 9) 95011380
@handmade.ecuador
HANDMADE
by InnTrend Co.
Hecho en Ecuador
Producido por: VIXITEX
Ruc: 1801748813001
NTE INEN 1875
www.inntrendco.com

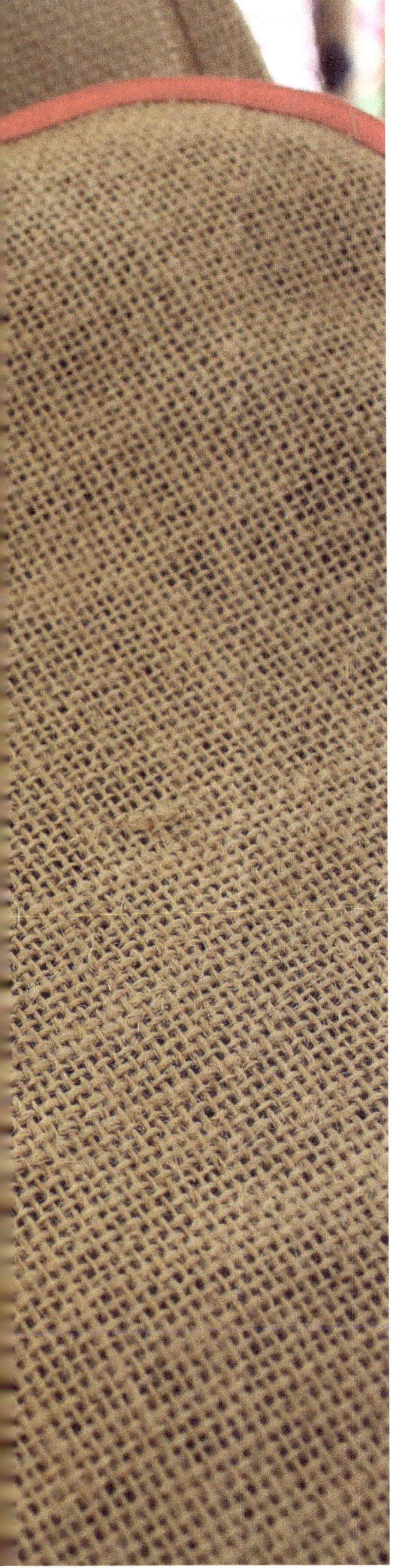

Prepare now your resin surface for work. Lite Pour-on High Gloss Finish I love Environtex! It turns whatever you create into a business piece!

Mix the resin in the Direction of the package.

Then pour directly into the middle of the tray.

Tilt the tray slightly to cover the whole base of the tray with the resin. Twenty minutes let it sit. Then use a butane torch or a heat pistol for popping any of the forming bubbles. Then cover with a card piece and let it heal overnight.

It's ready to use when the tray doesn't smell like resin!

Filler with a delicious breakfast, or use on the couch as a work surface. There are many ways to experience this fun tropical tray.

GOLD FOIL ROSE IRON-ON VINYL ON CRICUT STRAW BAG!

MATERIALS NEEDED

Cricut EasyPress 2
Cricut EasyPress
Rose Gold Foil Iron-on Vinyl
Cricut Maker
Cricut EasyPress Mat

DIRECTION

Place the rose gold sheet on the mat with the tile's shiny gold surface; look over the picture. Then cut the shape off in the right place. Excess vinyl should be removed and weeded.

Set it on the top of the bag with a bright side.

Remain firm while it presses inside the bag with towels.

Cover with a cover or Teflon board to prevent melting of the bag.

Set the EasyPress 2 at the correct material temperature. Pull down firmly while heating (Check this chart).

Let the project entirely refresh before the carrier plate is removed.

The bag is now ready to be gifted or filled!

CACTUS FAUX LEATHER CRICUT TOTE BAG!

MATERIALS NEEDED

Cricut maker or cutting machine
Green Feather Iron-on Vinyl
EasyPress 2 thin
Cricut Iron-on Protective pad
Cricut Design Space Directioncactus

DIRECTIONS

Place the iron on the side of the mat in color vinyl down to cut it.

Weed out excess plastic, cool 14 cactus.

I love the bright iron foil! Cut off all the cacti.

Then inside the fake leather tote, placed the EasyPress pad.

Line the cactus to know the distance for the finished product you want. The first one or three is then mounted.

The protective surface should be sealed.

Set the EasyPress 2 to the proper false leather con-

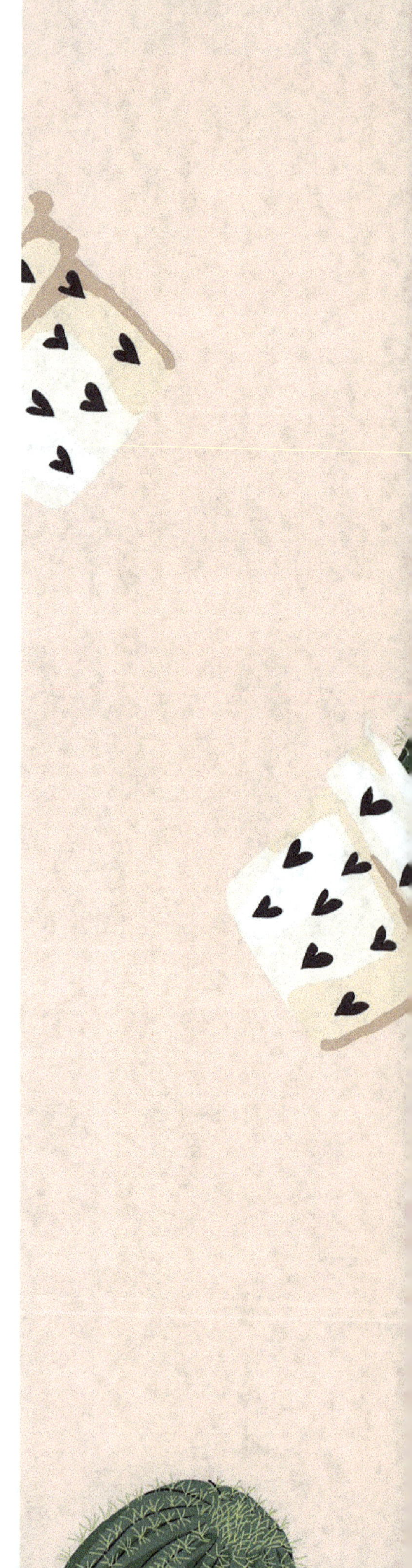

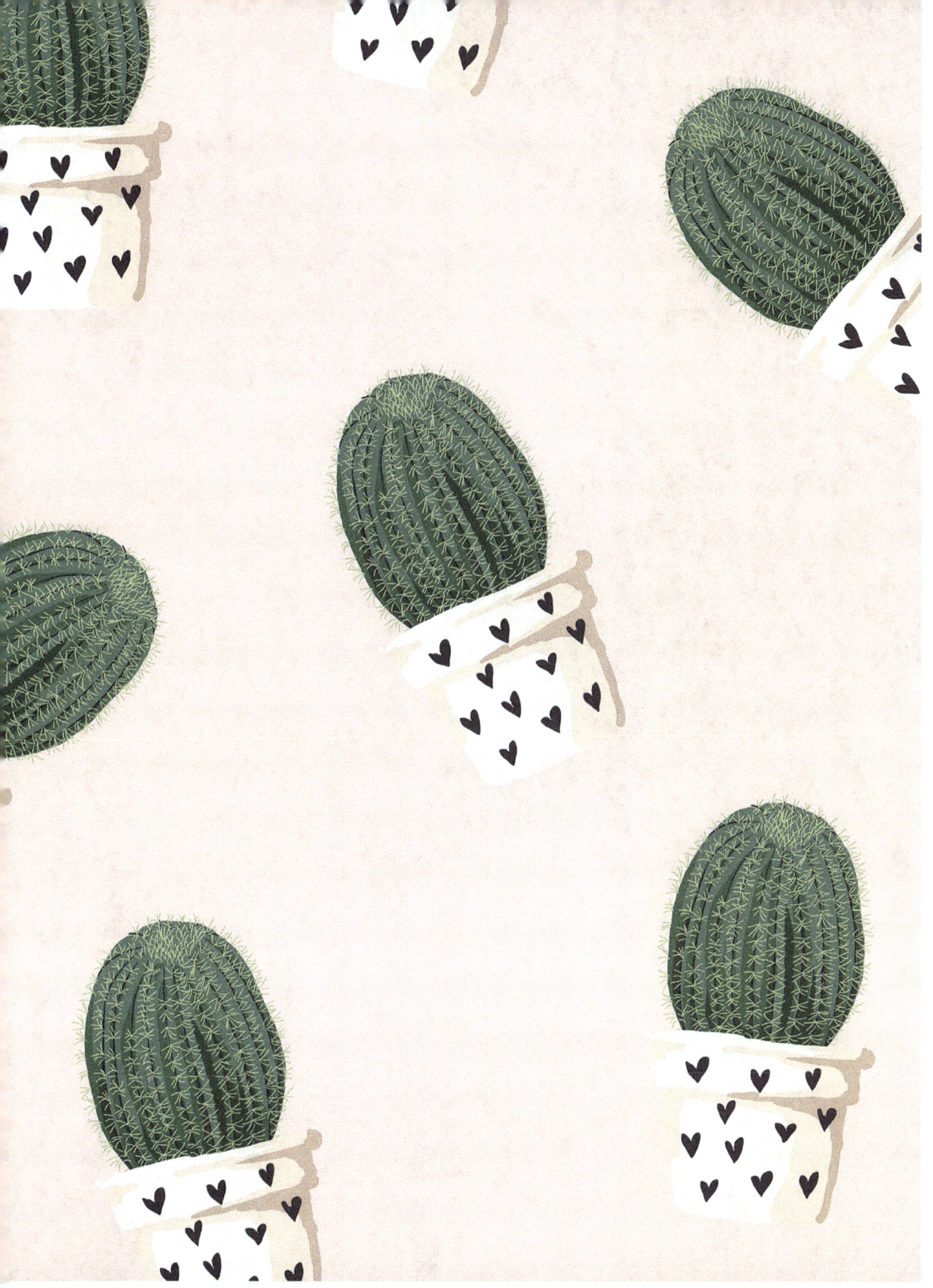

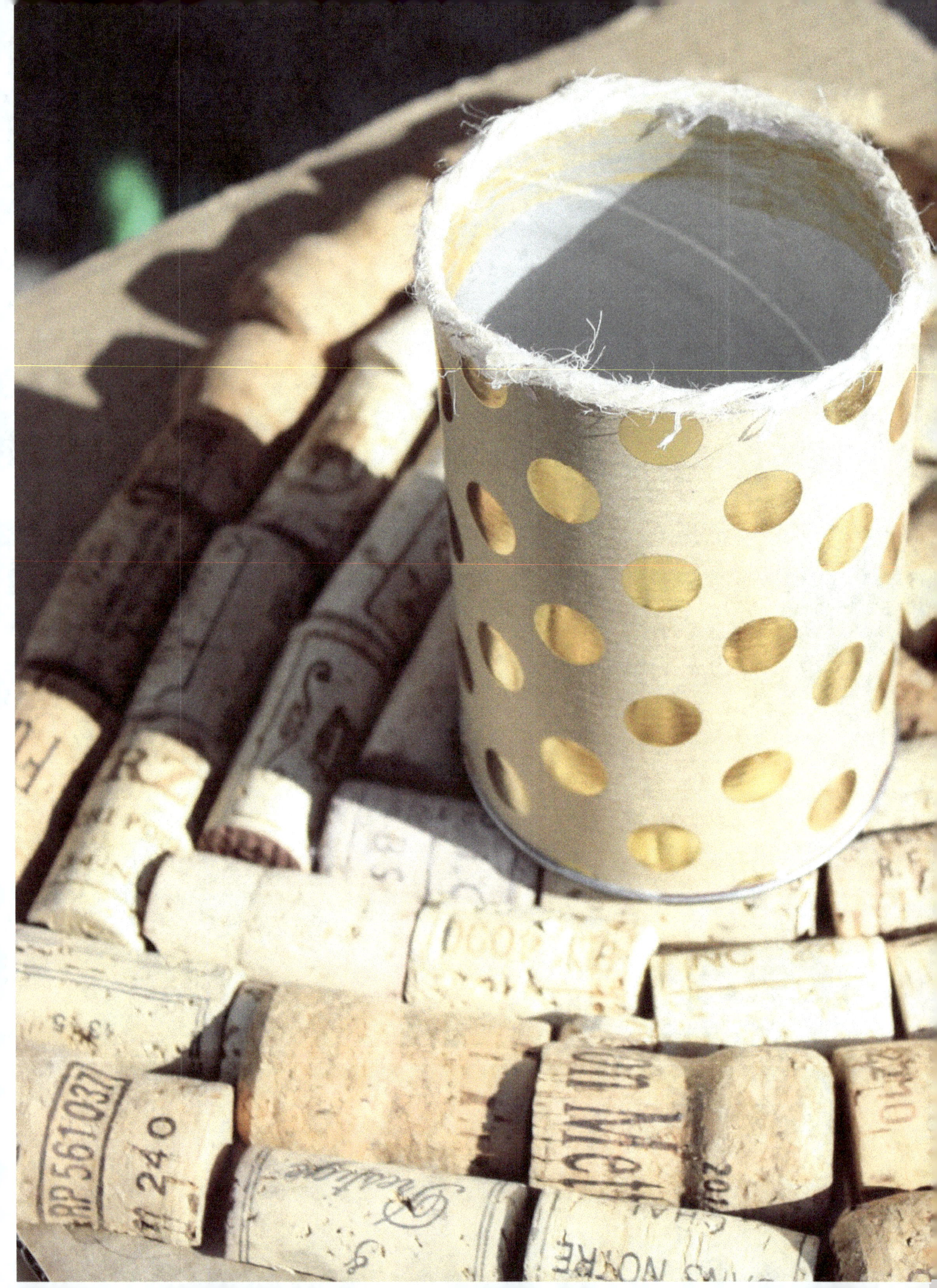

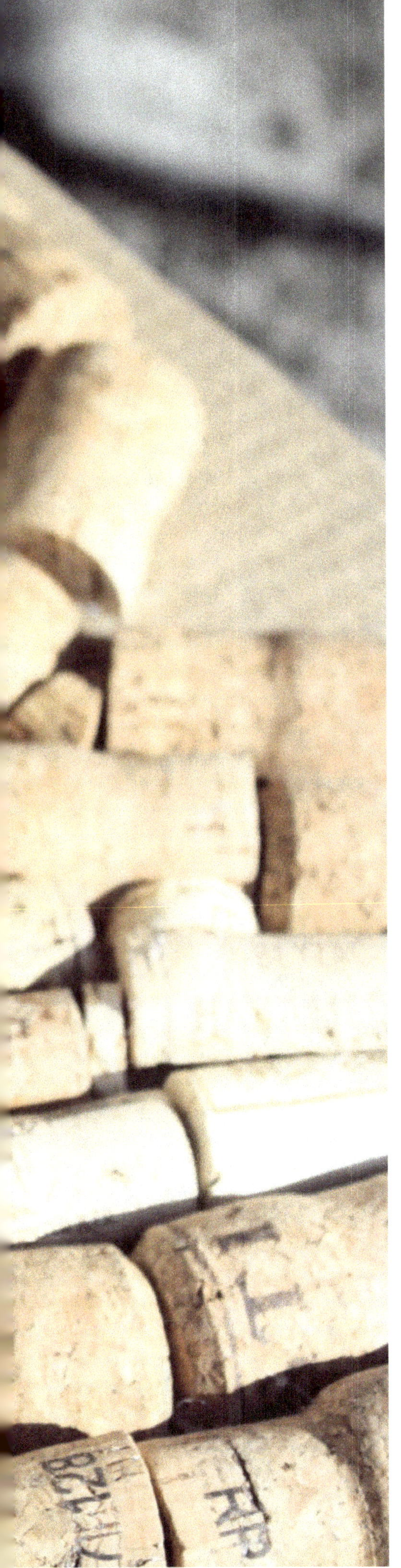

figuration. It can be slightly cooler at 295 to keep the tote from melting and squeezed at once for five seconds. Then another five seconds pulled. Tap on the EasyPress firmly.
Repeat for every cacti cluster.
Let the vinyl completely cool down, and then remove the plastic sheet from the container.
Simple, when cooled down, to peel off. Re-press if necessary if it doesn't look like it is adhered to.
Now the bag is ready to fill and remove from the city with all kinds of goodies. It's also a great homemade gift!

THE PEN HOLDER CLASP MINI LEATHER JOURNAL WITH CRICUT MAKER

MATERIALS NEEDED

Cricut EasyPress 2 Small
Cricut Iron-On Patent Protection
Mini Composition Book
Cricut Design Space

DIRECTIONS:

Slide in the mat and place in the holder the marking wheel. The first result of the project will be. Then remove a marker, and replace it with the fine blade. During this process, do not remove the mat. Simply replace the blade and press C.
You can cut out the forms fast and remove them from the mat.
Cut a few vinyl pictures out of iron. The pictures need only be 1.75 cm or less.

Heat up to 300° your EasyPress 2 and place the iron-on journal cover on the EasyPress mat.

Cover and press EasyPress 2 15 seconds. Cover with a protection plate. This is it! This is it!

Let the iron-on refresh fully... the carrier sheet then flake back.

It the time for cement rubber now.

Cut a faux leather scrap piece that covers the diary slits. Add the backside of the diary and the top side of the piece cut with rubber cement... do not put the slit on the piece.

Dry the cement rubber and cover the smaller piece with the slits.

Then put the cement on the top of the diary book and cover the inside of it. Tacky, let them dry.

Press the rubber cement book of the leather and then line up and press. Apply rubber cement to the back of the book and leather inside. No cement rubber between the lines scored. Allow the rubber cement to dry, and then pick and press.

Press firmly down to secure your book. The book will remain perfect until you have a new book of fillers to peel and glue off. Leather can be used again in this way!

Please fold over the top flap and insert in a slit loop a mini pen or a regular pen. It makes the journal's perfect fastening! Never sit down without a pen for writing or sketching.

This project only takes 15 minutes when Cricut Maker is set up and ready to go. That's the best handmade donation or stocking cushion!

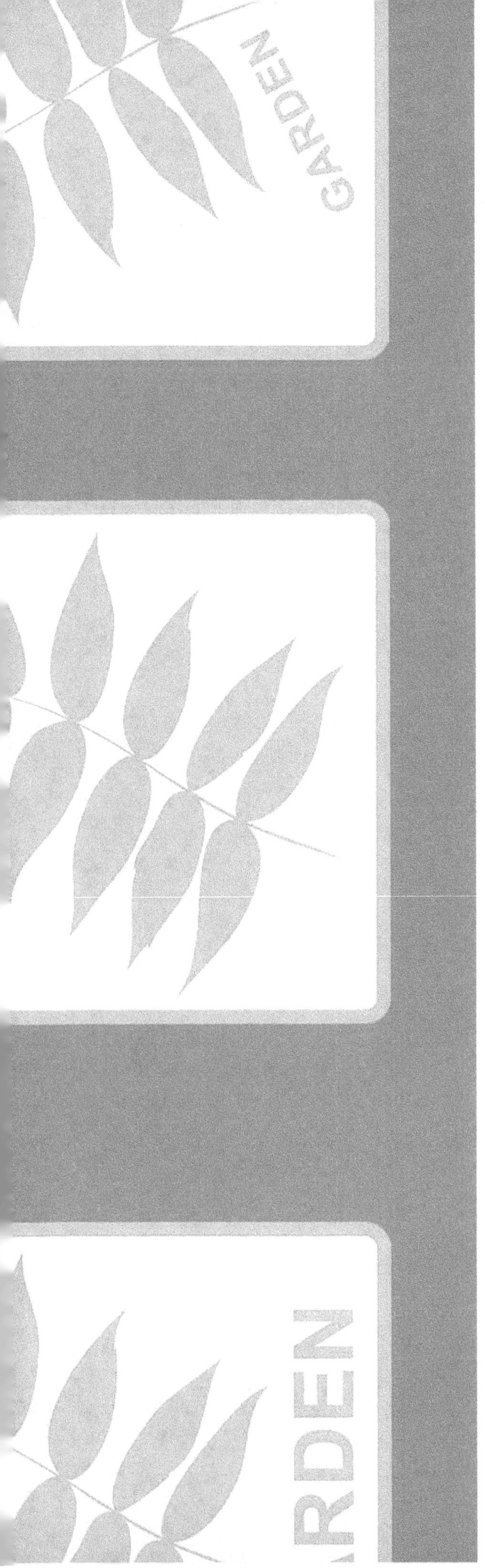

<u>LEATHER FOIL IRON-ON NAME GIFT TAG</u>
<u>CRICUT MAKER'S KEYCHAINS!</u>

MATERIALS NEEDED

Cricut Iron-on Foil in rose gold
Cricut EasyPress 2 Small
Cricut EasyPress Mat
Cricut Tools
Cricut True Control Knife
Cricut Self-Healing Mat
Keychain Lanyards
Cricut Normal and Strong Grip Cutting
Cricut Self-Healing
Cricut EasyPress 2 Small
Cricut EasyPress

DIRECTIONS:

Start by opening up Cricut Design Space
Design Space comes complete with many
fonts, pictures, and characteristics to be used
immediately after you plug into it. You can
easily upload your images, but the project
today will only use a Cricut fountain.
Create and open a textbox to a new canvas.
Specify your name, and in the drop-down list,
select the ZOO DAY font. The all-caps fonts
are perfect for this. It works great.   When
the name has been written down, the letter
space is decreased so that the letters start to
touch each other. Touch them before and
after each letter.
You can check out my project here, but your

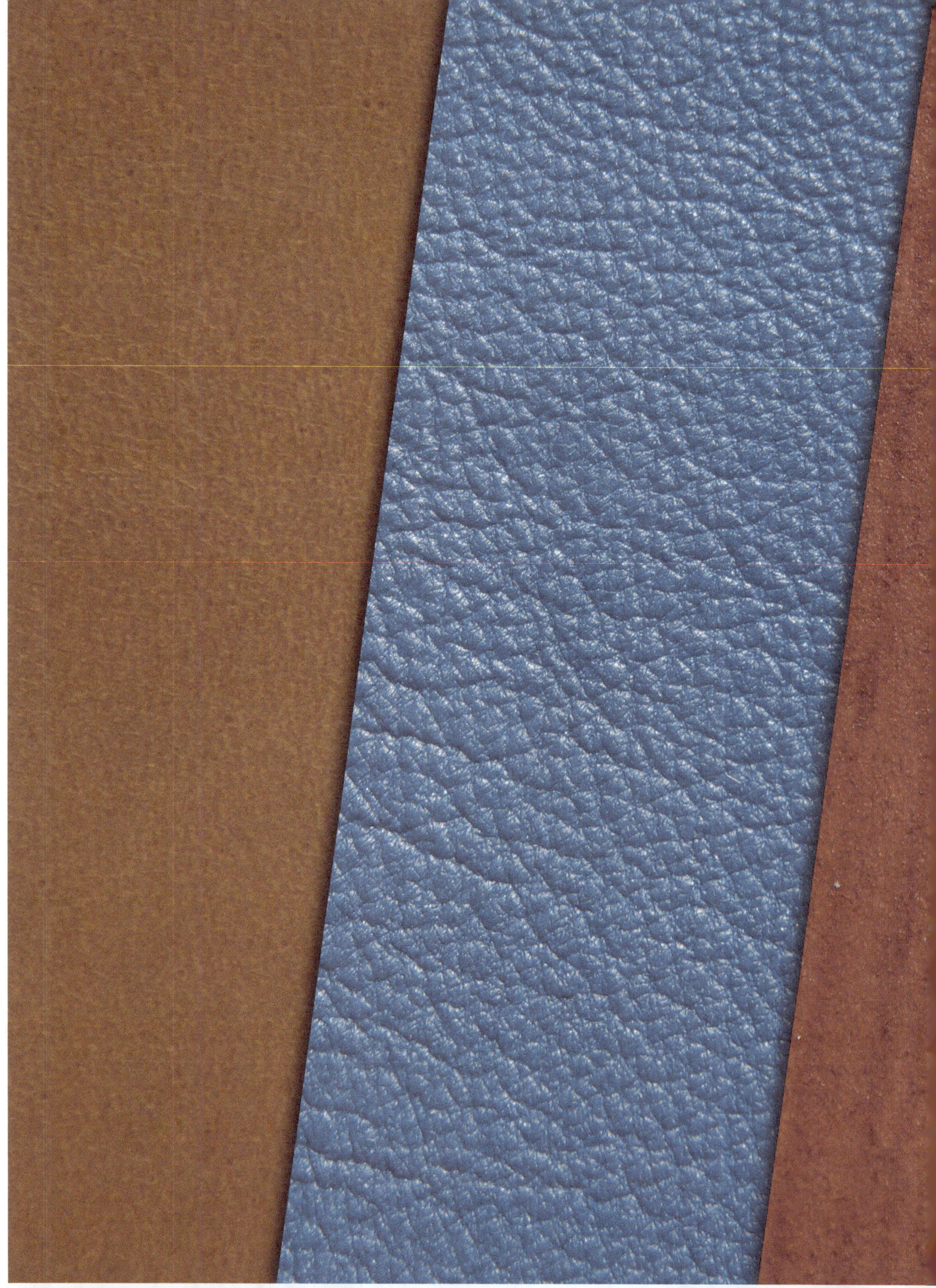

custom names must be created.

Make it visible to both layers.

Changing the iron-on vinyl color from the top layer to the color... or closing.

Double every name now.

The background of one version must be visible, the other the front.

Select and solder every single name. All letters will be merged into one solid piece.

After soldering, the background is substantial, and each name is reliable. Choose and sweat or join all the blue names. Repeat the yellow names are soldering.

Click on the button to make it.

On two separate mats, you will bring up the sold or attached words.

Mirror the front-end mat picture. Then, with a glittering side, place the iron-on vinyl on your mat. Set the Iron-on Foil configuration of the machine.

Click on the "C" button and insert it into the Cricut Maker. It will cut the picture with the fine dot blade beautifully.

Remove the vinyl iron and trim the edges once cut. Set it above your Bright Pad Cricut and see where you should weed. It has a breeze. To remove excess vinyl, use the weeding tool.

Get the leather ready for the second mat. Leather cutting was never so comfortable with the Blade and the Builder Knife.

To help protect your cutting mat against leather, use contact paper. Remove the leather packaging and turn it roughly onto it.

Place the paper and securely paste it on clear contact paper. Cut the leather in plastic.

Slide onto the machine and put the chrome blade

in the machine to the right.
Make sure you have calibrated the blade befo-
rehand.
Put the leather-covered contact paper right on
the strong grip mat.
Place the blade in the Cricut Maker and have a
chrome blade quickly cut the leather.

ROSE GOLD LEATHER EARRINGS DIY

MATERIALS NEEDED

Cricut Maker
Cricut Strong Grip Mat
Clear Contact Paper
Cricut Metalic Rose Gold Vinyl
Cricut tools
Hook and jump rings
Critical Metal leather Gold Cricut

DIRECTIONS:

Start by stitching a clear contact paper to the
backside of the leather. This keeps everything
from the matt surface and keeps the mat more
useful. Place the leather on the strong grip mat
(contact paper side down).
To design a rope shape with a tiny hole cut at
the top, use Cricut Design Space. Cut it off, then.
I shouted. I was using the blade for the knife, but
I was too tired to switch to it.
And the leather wasn't cut all around its rear
edge, so there's a bit of fluff. I cut it off with
the scissors of Cricut.

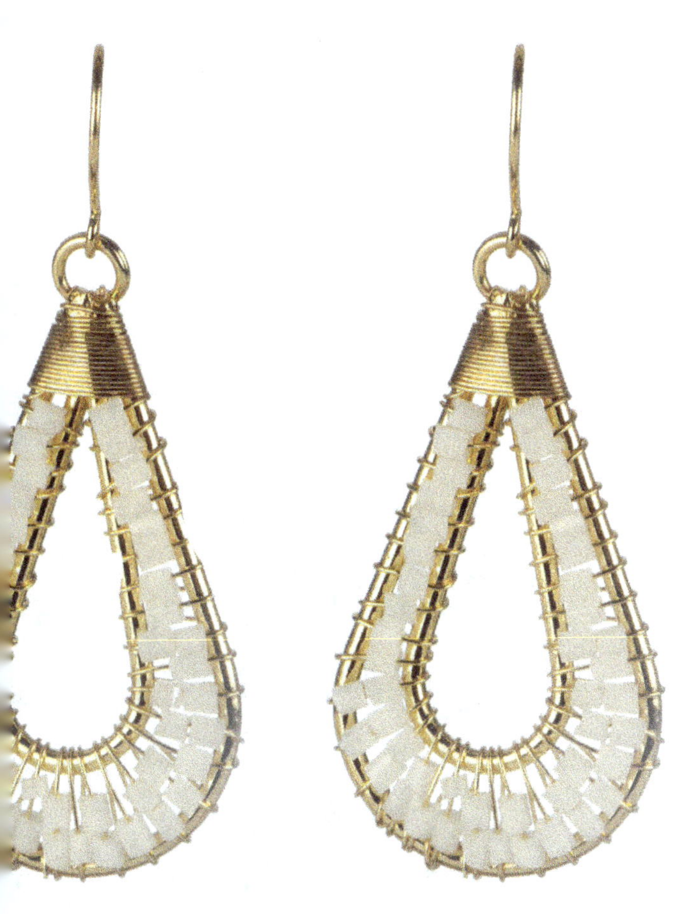

Then use some pins to attach a hook to the leather earring.

Cut some sweet shapes out of metallic rose vinyl gold. These are the forms in the Cricut Access file I found on a CDS.

Then peel the leather and stick it to the back. The rose-gold and rose-gold vinyl go hand in hand.

Under the layers of leather, hit metallic.

Such a simple DIY on an excellent declaration pair of earrings.

Chapter 2
Fabric and textiles projects

TASSELS

MATERIALS NEEDED

12" x 18" fabric rectangles
Fabric mat
Glue gun

DIRECTION

Open Cricut Design Space and create a new project.
Select the "Image" button in the lower left-hand corner and search "tassel."
Select the image of a rectangle with lines on each side and click "Insert."
Place the fabric on the cutting mat.
Send the design to the Cricut.
Remove the fabric from the mat, saving the extra square.
Place the fabric face down and begin rolling tightly, starting on the uncut side. Untangle the fringe as needed.
Use some of the scrap fabric and a hot glue gun to secure the tassel at the top.
Decorate whatever you want with your new tassels!

MONOGRAMMED DRAWSTRING BAG

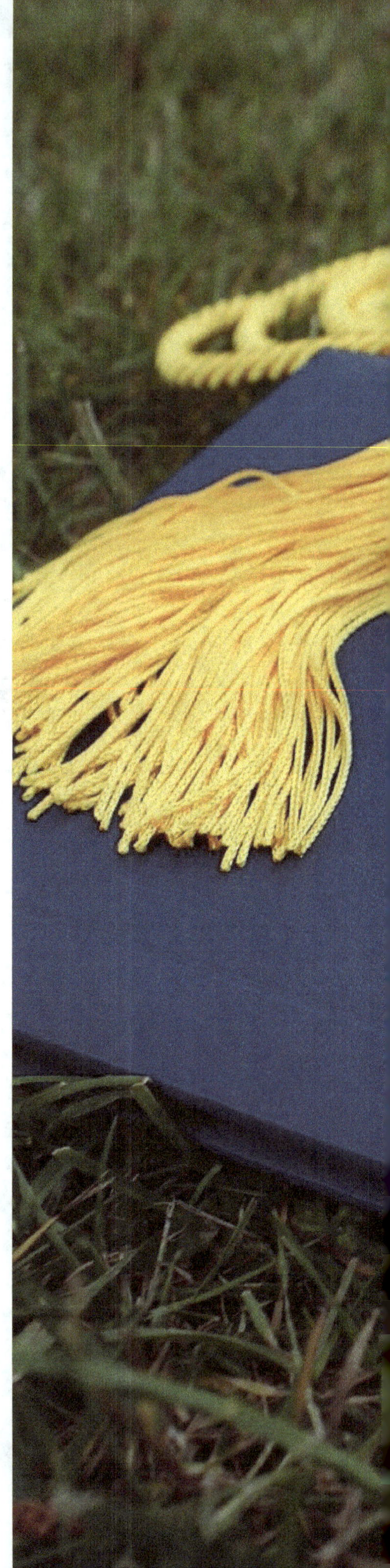

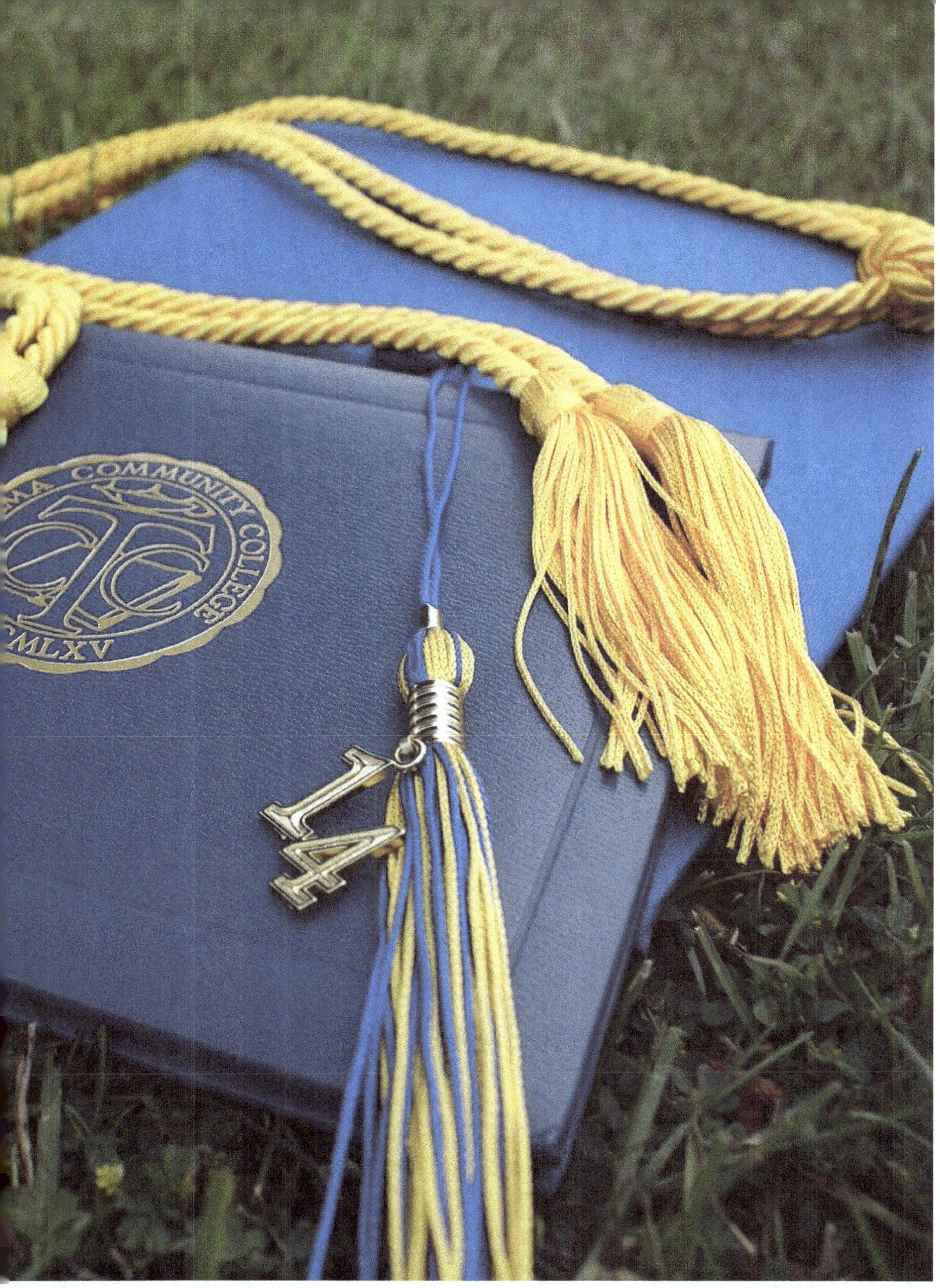

COMMUNITY COLLEGE
MLXV
14

MATERIALS NEEDED

Two matching rectangles of fabric
Needle and thread
Ribbon
Heat transfer vinyl
Cricut EasyPress or iron
Cutting mat
Weeding tool or pick

DIRECTION

Open Cricut Design Space and create a new project.
Select the "Image" button in the lower left-hand corner and search "monogram."
Select the monogram of your choice and click "Insert."
Place the iron-on material shiny liner side down on the cutting mat.
Send the design to the Cricut.
Use the weeding tool or pick to remove excess material.
Remove the monogram from the mat.
Center the monogram on your fabric, then move it a couple of inches down so that it won't be folded up when the ribbon is drawn.
Iron the design onto the fabric.
Place the two rectangles together, with the outer side of the fabric facing inward.
Sew around the edges, leaving a seam allowance.
Leave the top open and stop a couple of inches down from the top.

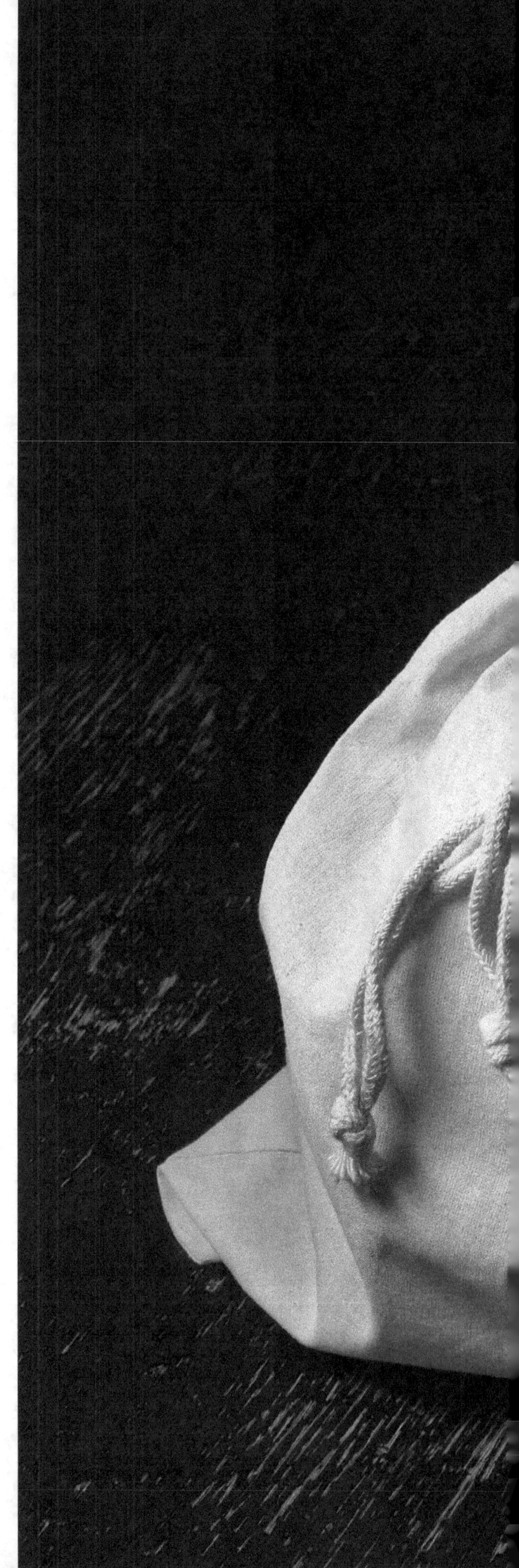

Fold the top of the bag down until you reach your stitches.

Sew along the bottom of the folded edge, leaving the sides open.

Turn the bag right side out.

Thread the ribbon through the loop around the top of the bag.

Use your new drawstring bag to carry what you need

PAW PRINT SOCKS

MATERIALS NEEDED

Socks
Heat transfer vinyl
Cutting mat
Scrap cardboard
Weeding tool or pick
Cricut EasyPress or iron

DIRECTION

Open Cricut Design Space and create a new project.

Select the "Image" button in the lower left-hand corner and search "paw prints."

Select the paw prints of your choice and click "Insert."

Place the iron-on material on the mat.

Send the design to the Cricut.

Use the weeding tool or pick to remove excess material.

Remove the material from the mat.

Fit the scrap cardboard inside of the socks.
Place the iron-on material on the bottom of the socks.
Use the EasyPress to adhere it to the iron-on material.
After cooling, remove the cardboard from the socks.
Wear your cute paw print socks!

NIGHT SKY PILLOW

MATERIALS NEEDED

Black, dark blue, or dark purple fabric
Heat transfer vinyl in gold or silver
Cutting mat
Polyester batting
Weeding tool or pick
Cricut EasyPress

DIRECTION

Decide the shape you want for your pillow, and cut two matching shapes out of the fabric.
Open Cricut Design Space and create a new project.
Select the "Image" button in the lower left-hand corner and search "stars."
Select the stars of your choice and click "Insert."
Place the iron-on material on the mat.
Send the design to the Cricut.
Use the weeding tool or pick to remove excess material.

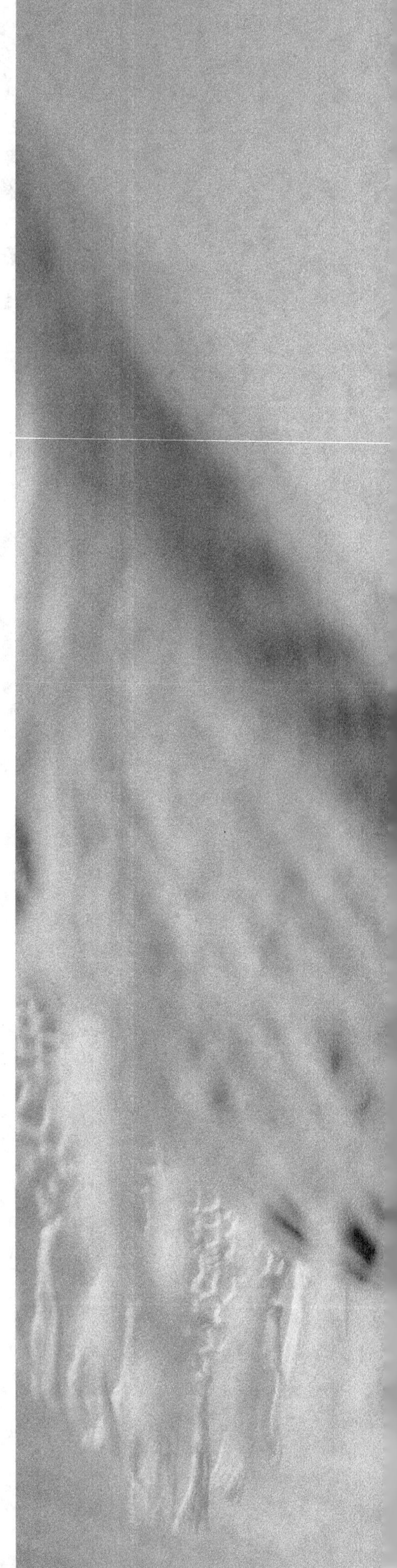

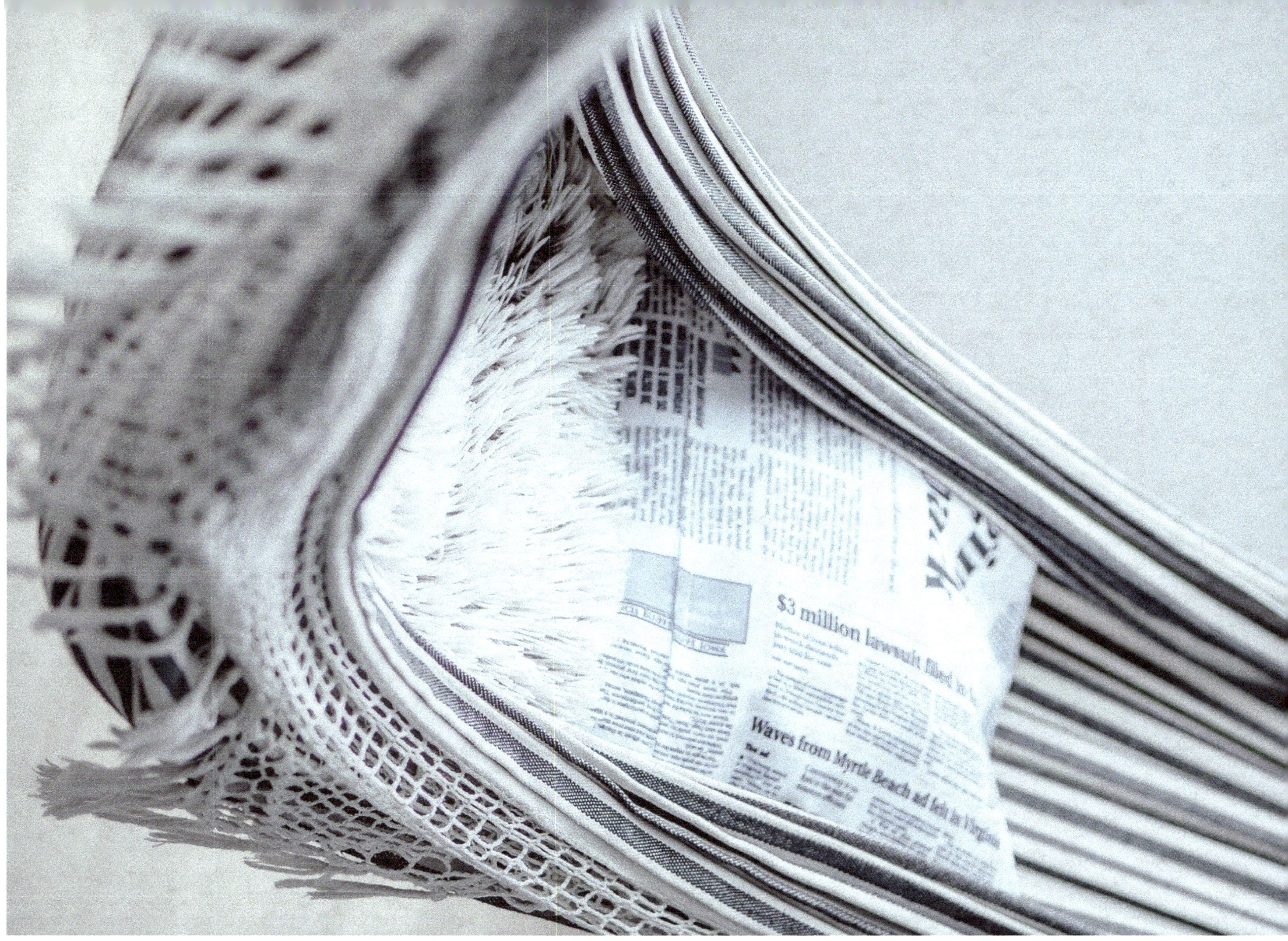

$3 million lawsuit filed in
Waves from Myrtle Beach

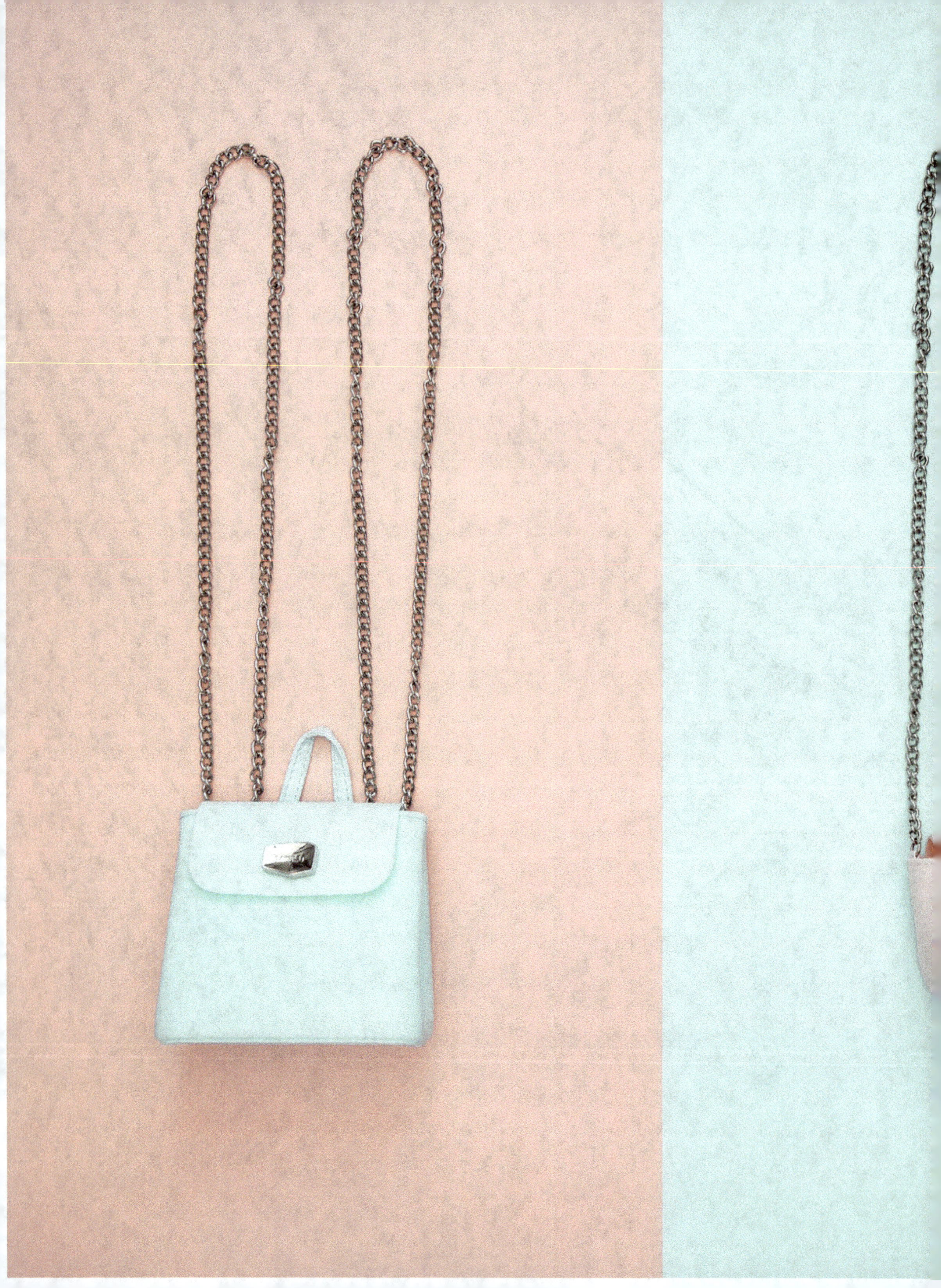

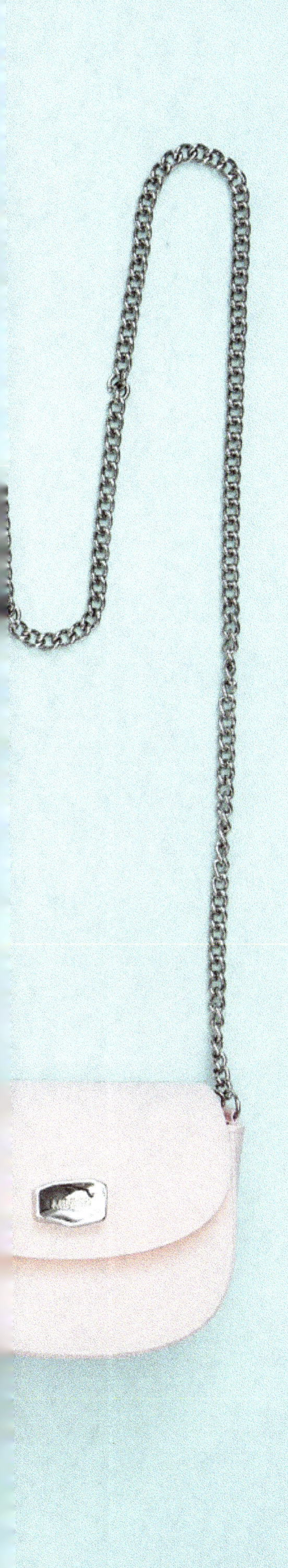

Remove the material from the mat.
Place the iron-on material on the fabric.
Use the EasyPress to adhere it to the iron-on material.
Sew the two fabric pieces together, leaving allowance for a seam and a small space open.
Fill the pillow with polyester batting through the small open space.
Sew the pillow shut
Cuddle up to your starry pillow!

CLUTCH PURSE

MATERIALS NEEDED

Two fabrics, one for the exterior and one for the
Fusible interior fleece
Fabric cutting mat
D-ring
Sew-on snap
Lace
Zipper
Sewing machine
Fabric scissors
Keychain or charm of your choice

DIRECTION

Open Cricut Design Space and create a new project.
Select the "Image" button in the lower left-hand corner and search for "essential wallet."
Select the basic wallet template and click "Insert."
Place the fabric on the mat.

Send the design to the Cricut.

Remove the fabric from the mat.

Attach the fusible fleecing to the wrong side of the exterior fabric.

Attach lace to the edges of the exterior fabric.

Assemble the D-ring strap.

Place the D-ring onto the strap and sew it into place.

Fold the pocket pieces wrong side out over the top of the zipper, and sew it into place.

Fold the pocket's wrong side in and sew the sides.

Sew the snap onto the pocket.

Lay the pocket on the right side of the main fabric lining so that the corners of the pocket's bottom are behind the lining fabric's curved edges. Sew the lining piece to the zipper tape.

Fold the lining behind the pocket and iron in place.

Sew on the other side of the snap.

Trim the zipper so that it's not overhanging the edge.

Sew the two pocket layers to the exterior fabric across the bottom.

Sew around all of the layers.

Trim the edges with fabric scissors.

Turn the clutch almost entirely inside out and sew the opening closed.

Turn the clutch inside out and press the corners into place.

Attach your charm or keychain to the zipper.

Carry your new clutch wherever you need it!

EASY LACEY DRESS

MATERIALS NEEDED

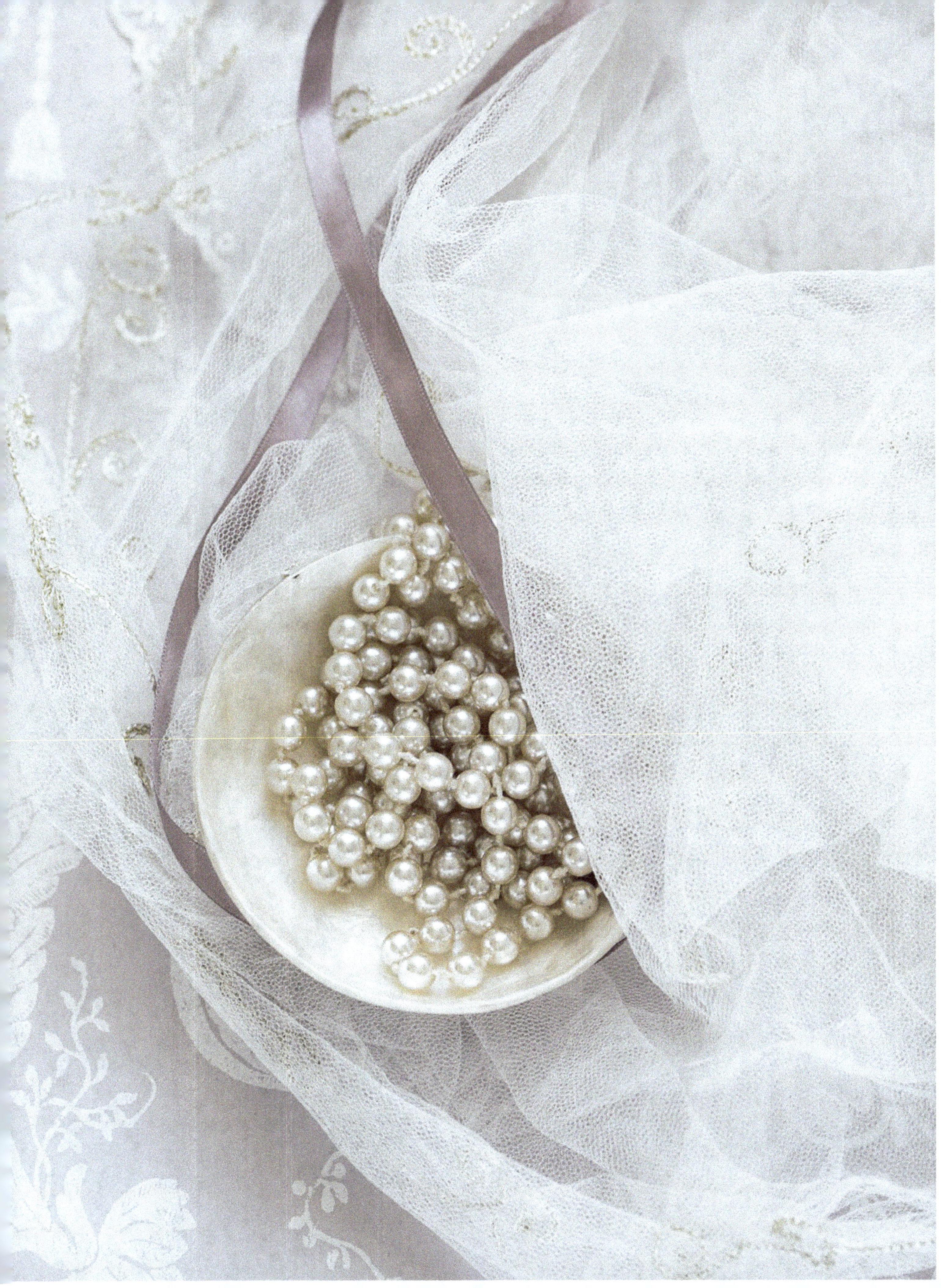

Dress of your choice
White heat transfer vinyl
Cricut EasyPress or iron
Cutting mat
Weeding tool or pick

DIRECTION

Open Cricut Design Space and create a new project.
Select the "Image" button in the lower left-hand corner and search "vintage lace border."
Choose your favorite lace border and click "Insert."
Place your vinyl on the cutting mat.
Send the design to your Cricut.
Use a weeding tool or pick to remove the excess vinyl from the design.
Place the design along the hem of the dress with the plastic side up. Add lace wherever you like, such as along the collar or sleeves.
Carefully iron on the design.
After cooling, peel away the plastic by rolling it.
Dress your child up in her adorable lacey dress!

DINOSAUR T-SHIRT

MATERIALS NEEDED

T-shirt of your choice
Green heat transfer vinyl
Cricut EasyPress or iron
Cutting mat
Weeding tool or pick

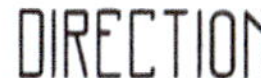

DIRECTION

Open Cricut Design Space.
Select the "Image" button in the lower left-hand corner and search "dinosaur."
Choose your favorite dinosaur and click "Insert."
Select "Image" again and search for "fossils."
Choose your favorite fossil and click "Insert."
Copy the fossil once so that you have two of them.
Place your vinyl on the cutting mat.
Send the design to your Cricut.
Use a weeding tool or pick to remove the excess vinyl from the design.
Place the dinosaur in the center of the t-shirt, and a fossil on each sleeve, with the plastic side up.
Carefully iron on the design.
After cooling, peel away the plastic by rolling it.

FLOWER GARDEN TOTE BAG

MATERIALS NEEDED

Canvas tote bag
White heat transfer vinyl
Cricut EasyPress or iron
Cutting mat
Weeding tool or pick

DIRECTION

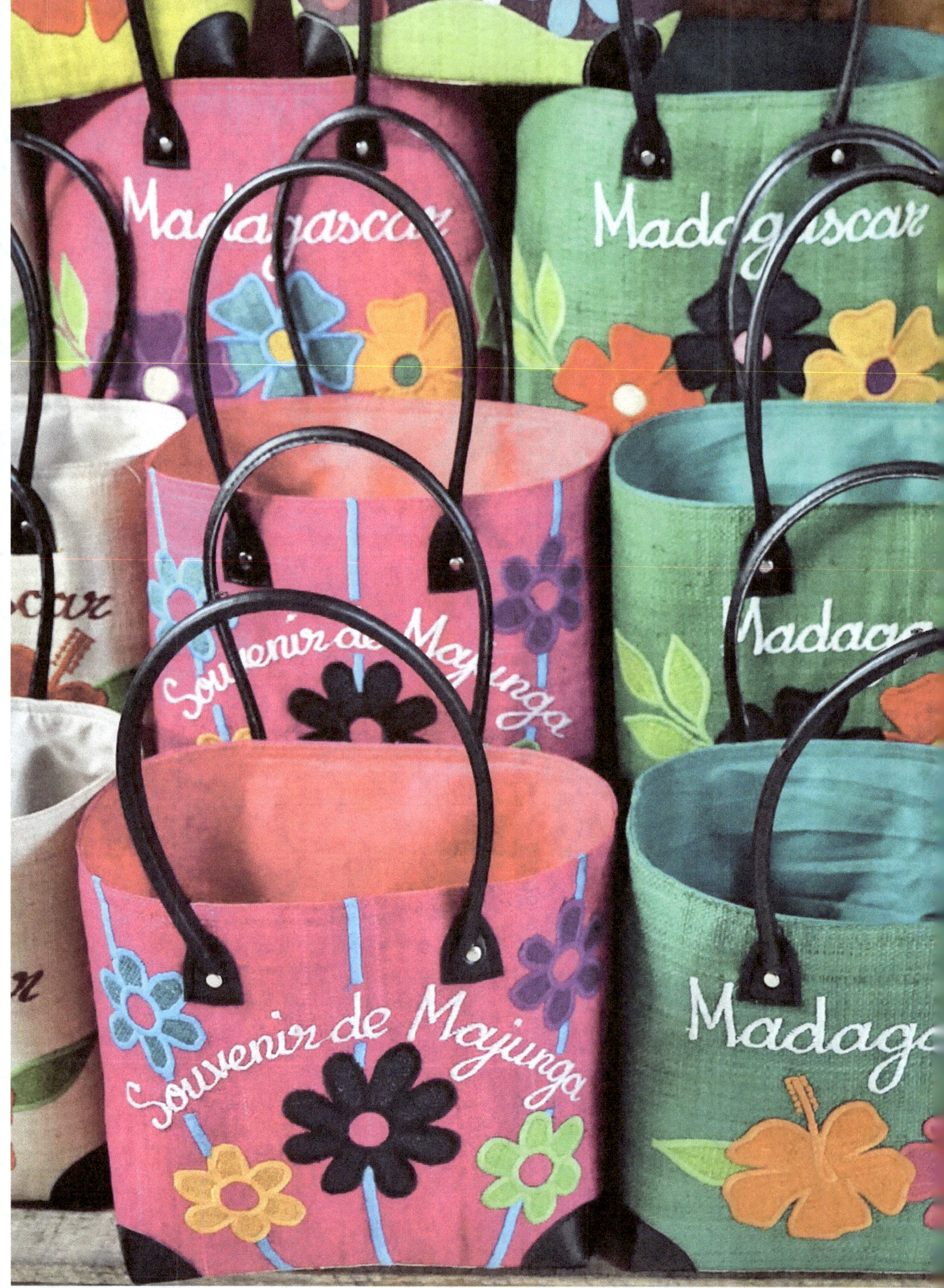

Madagascar
Madagascar
scar
Madaga
Souvenir de Majunga
Souvenir de Majunga
Madaga
n

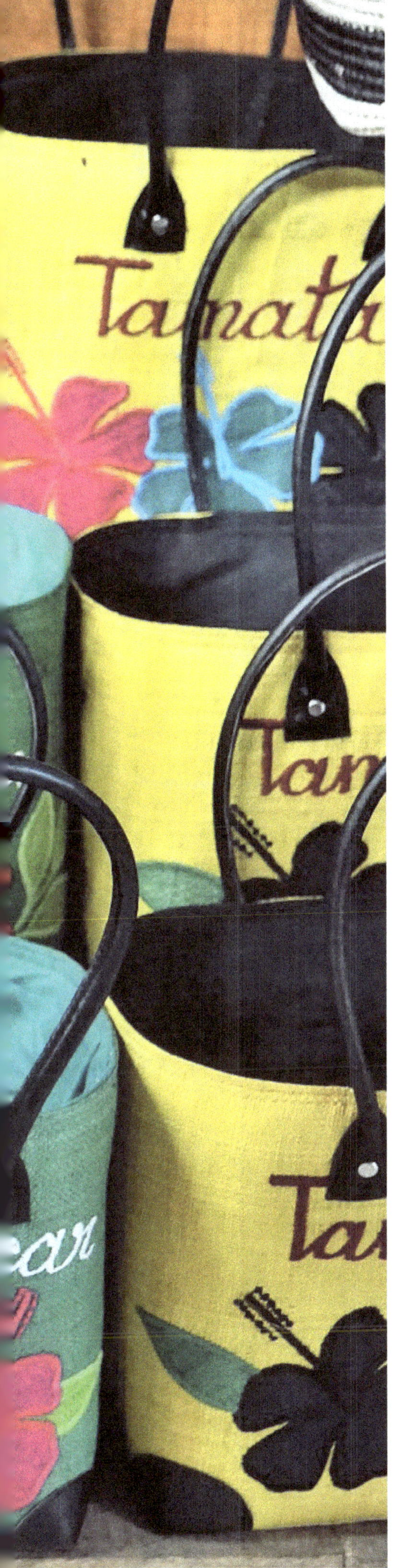

Open Cricut Design Space and create a new project.

Select the "Image" button in the lower left-hand corner and search "flowers."

Choose your favorite flower and click "Insert."

Continue with various flowers, lining them up together to form a straight edge at the bottom.

Place your vinyl on the cutting mat.

Send the design to your Cricut.

Use a weeding tool or pick to remove the excess vinyl from the design.

Place the design along the bottom of the tote bag with the plastic
side up.

Carefully iron on the design.

After cooling, peel away the plastic by rolling it.

Carry around your new garden tote bag!

Chapter 3

Home décor projects

CLOUD SHELF

MATERIALS NEEDED

Créalia "Clouds" wooden shelf
Acrylic tube 120 matt white
3u7m, bkjFlat synthetic brush n ° 18
Straight scissors - 17 cm
Transparent ruler for creative hobbies .30 cm
Precision cutter and three blades
Self-healing cutting mat - 45x35 cm
Cardboard Stickers - Baby
Extra strong double-sided adhesive tape - 6mm x 10m

DIRECTION

Paint the cloud shelf white. Let dry.
Download and transfer the templates to different papers from the collection and compose the decoration.
Glue the cut papers on the cloud shelf using the extra-strong double-sided tape.
Personalize the shelf with stickers from the collection.
Tip: the 30 x 30 cm block of paper offers visuals to frame to decorate your child's room or make scrapbooking albums.
The cloud shelf is ready to decorate your child's

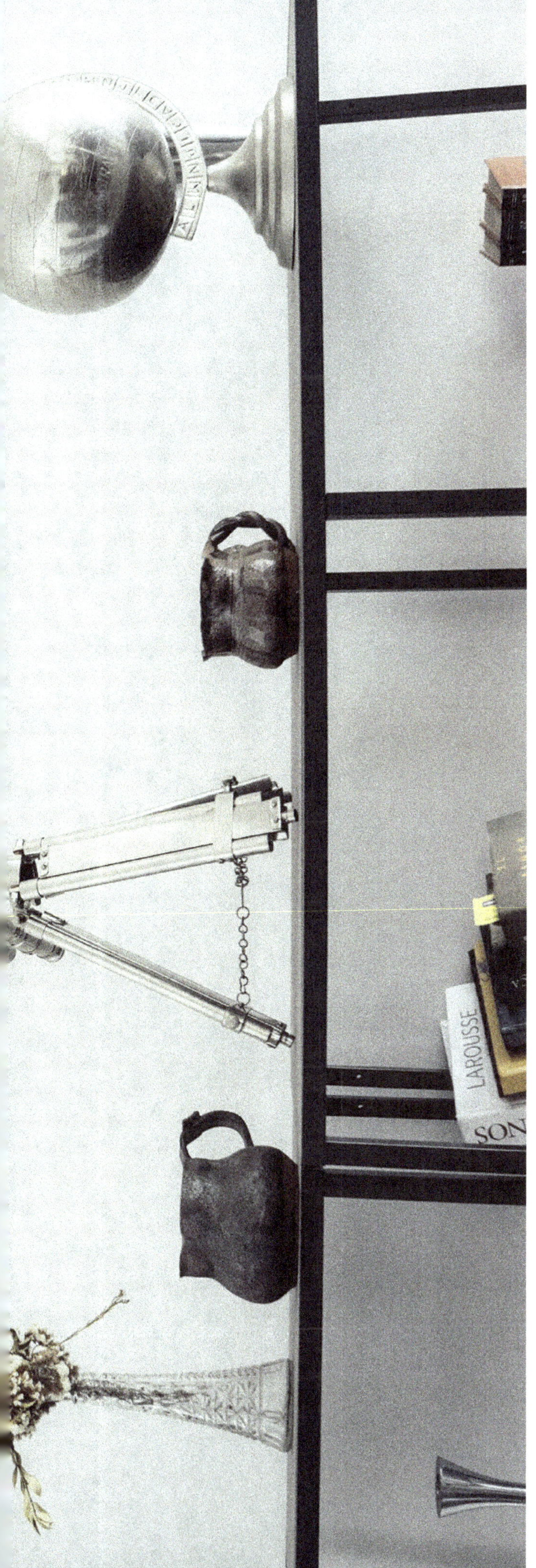

room

HANDMADE FRAME

MATERIAL NEEDED

Cricut Explore Air 2 Cutting Equipment
Standard Fixing Cutting Base - Cricut (Green Cutting Base);
Tool Kit with Champagne Guillotine - Cricut - 09 pieces ;
Transparent Acetate - Cricut - 30x30cm- 06 sheets ;
Copper Metallic Adhesive Vinyl - Cricut - 30x122cm - 01 unit ;
Kraft Paper ;
Kit Corrugated Cardboard and Plain Pastel - Cricut- 30x30cm - 20 sheets ;
Silicone Glue for Crafts;
Decorative Picture Frame (I used one in copper color).
Rope

DIRECTION

First, you will use the Cricut Explore Air 2 and the Cricut Green Cutting Base to cut two acetate sheets to the ideal size to stick behind the frame inside it.
Then it's time to cut out the details of the leaflets on the papers and the words on the adhesive vinyl. I used the Cricut Spalula and Hooked to shave everything, which goes in the Tool Kit with Champagne Guillotine - Cri-

cut - 09 pieces.

Then, using the silicone glue, you glue the paper sheets onto the second acetate sheet. After that, apply the cut words on the adhesive vinyl.

And finally, glue this acetate sheet already assembled behind the other, inside the frame; that is, the collages will be between the two acetate sheets. For a better finish, I stuck a string inside the edges.

ETCHED MONOGRAMMED GLASS

MATERIALS NEEDED

A glass of your choice - make sure that the spot you want to monogram is smooth
Vinyl
Cutting mat
Weeding tool or pick
Glass etching cream

DIRECTIONS

Open Cricut Design Space and create a new project.
Select the "Image" button in the Design Panel and search for "monogram."
Choose your favorite monogram and click "Insert."
Place your vinyl on the cutting mat.
Send the design to your Cricut.
Use a weeding tool or pick to remove the monogram, leaving the vinyl around it.
Remove the vinyl from the mat.
Carefully apply the vinyl around your glass, making it as smooth as possible, particularly around the

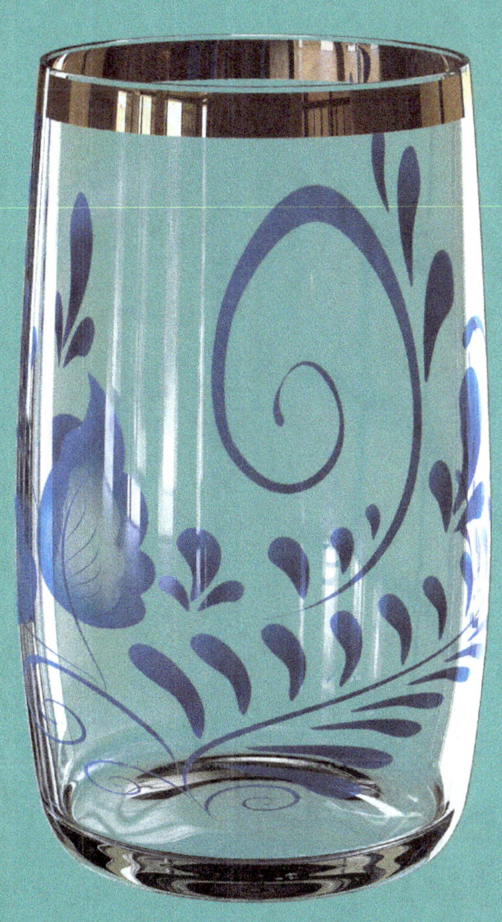

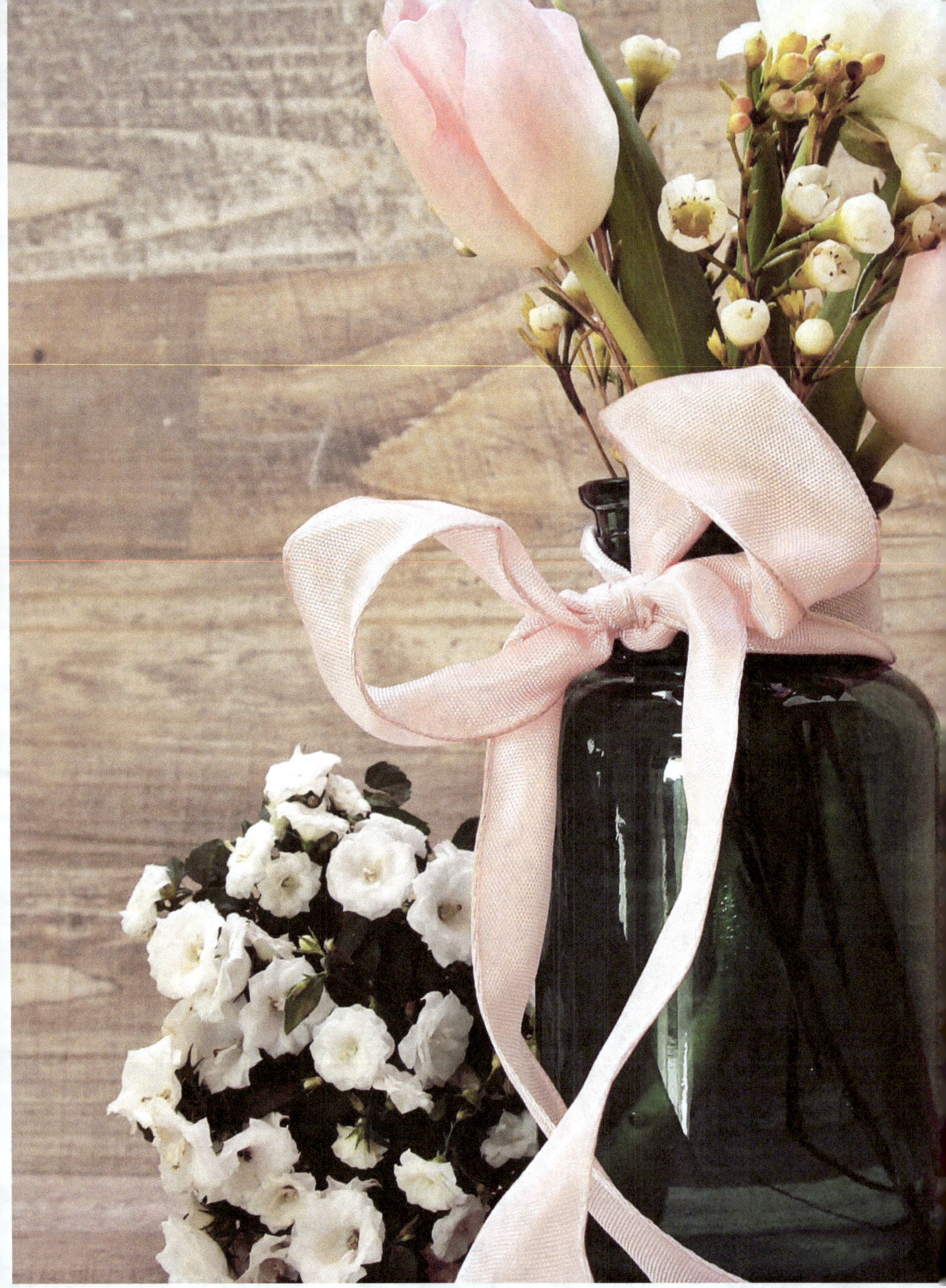

monogram.

If you have any letters with holes in your monogram, carefully reposition those cutouts in their proper place.

Following the Directions for the etching cream, apply it to your monogram.

Remove the cream and then the vinyl.

Give your glass a good wash.

Enjoy drinking out of your etched glass!

LIVE. LOVE. LAUGH GLASS BLOCK

MATERIALS NEEDED

Glass block
Frost spray paint
Clear enamel spray
Holographic vinyl
Vinyl transfer tape
Cutting mat
Weeding tool or pick
Fairy lights

DIRECTIONS

Spray the entire glass block with frost spray paint, and let it dry.

Spray the glass block with a coat of clear enamel spray, and let it dry.

Open Cricut Design Space and create a new project.

Select the "Text" button in the Design Panel.

Type "Live Love Laugh" in the text box.

Use the dropdown box to select your favorite font.

Arrange the words to sit on top of each other.
Place your vinyl on the cutting mat.
Send the design to your Cricut.
Use a weeding tool or pick to remove the excess vinyl from the design.
Apply transfer tape to the design.
Remove the paper backing and apply the words to the glass block.
Smooth down the design and carefully remove the transfer tape.
Place fairy lights in the opening of the block, leaving the battery pack on the outside.
Enjoy your decorative quote!

UNICORN WINE GLASS

MATERIALS NEEDED

Stemless wine glasses
Outdoor vinyl in the color of your choice
Vinyl transfer tape
Cutting mat
Weeding tool or pick
Extra fine glitter in the color of your choice
Mod Podge

DIRECTIONS

Open Cricut Design Space and create a new project.
Select the "Text" button in the Design Panel.
Type "It's not drinking alone if my unicorn is here."
Using the dropdown box, select your favorite font.
Adjust the positioning of the letters, rotating some

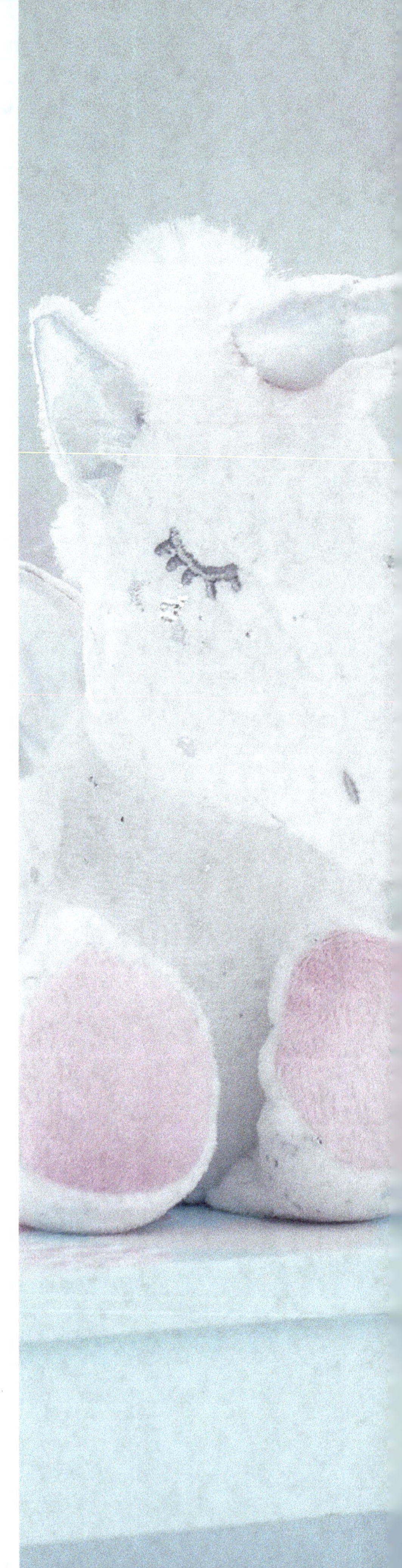

to give a whimsical look.

Select the "Image" button on the Design Panel and search for "unicorn."

Select your favorite unicorn and click "Insert," then arrange your design how you want it on the glass.

Place your vinyl on the cutting mat, making sure it is smooth and making full contact.

Send the design to your Cricut.

Use a weeding tool or pick to remove the excess vinyl from the design. Use the Cricut BrightPad to help if you have one.

Apply transfer tape to the design, pressing firmly and making sure there are no bubbles.

Remove the paper backing and apply the words to the glass where you'd like them. Leave at least a couple of inches at the bottom for the glitter. Smooth down the design and carefully remove the transfer tape.

Coat the bottom of the glass in Mod Podge, wherever you would like glitter to be. Give the area a wavy edge.

Sprinkle glitter over the Mod Podge, working quickly before it dries.

Add another layer of Mod Podge and glitter, and set it aside to dry.

Cover the glitter in a thick coat of Mod Podge.

Allow the glass to cure for at least 48 hours.

Enjoy drinking from your unicorn wine glass!

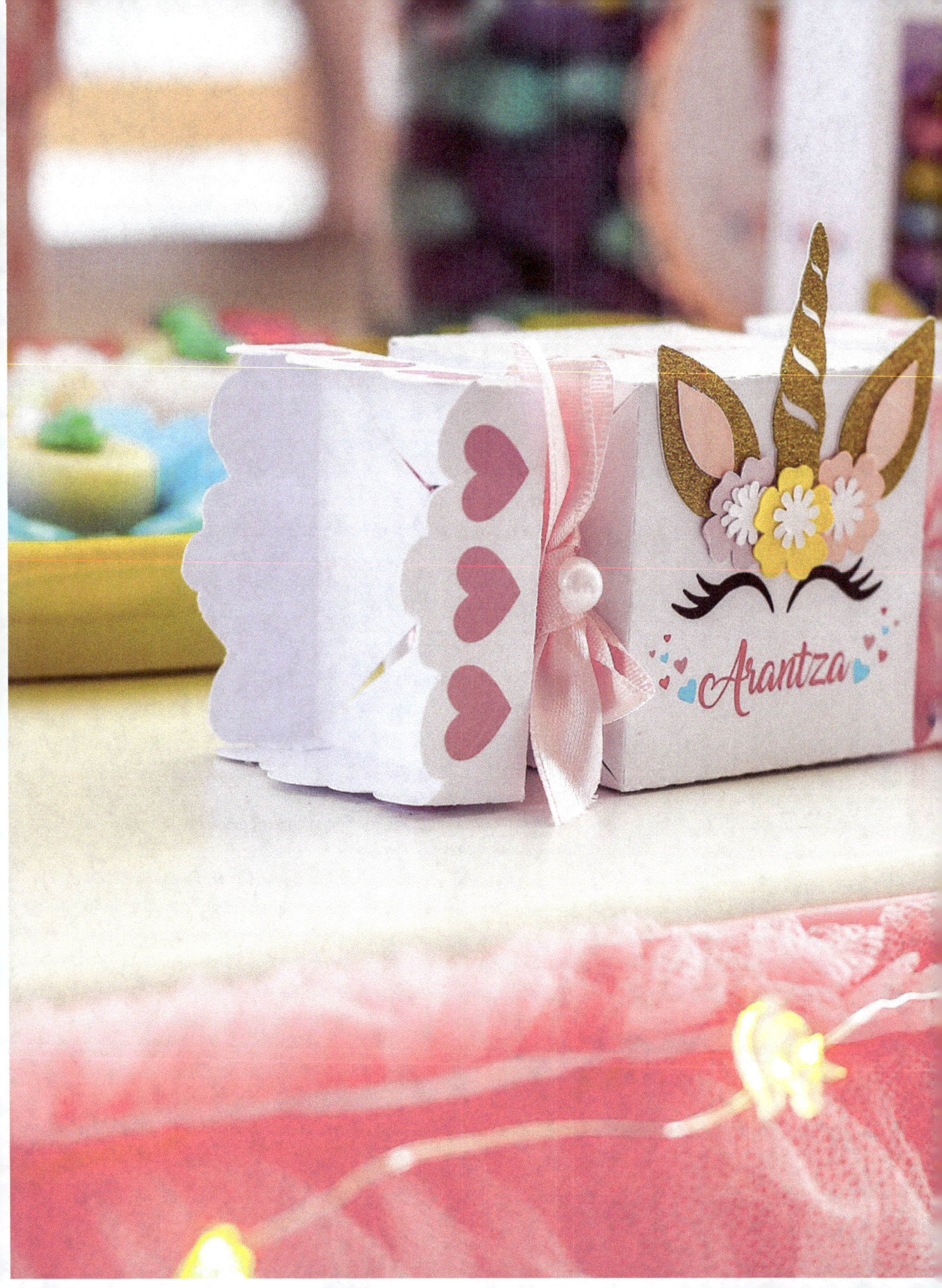
Arantza

Chapter 4

Projects for your family

A CUTE UNICORN BOX

MATERIALS NEEDED

The old box you'd prefer to make new
Craft paint
Glitter paint
Mod Podge - we love Mod Podge for a wide range of projects!
Paintbrushes in an assortment of sizes
Sprinkles, sparkle, and sweet sprinkles (you won't eat these, however)
Clay - we utilized stove prepare mud - air dry earth would work as well.
Glue to apply the horn
Spray sealer - discretionary
Supplies you have to brighten your unicorn box

DIRECTIONS

Allow the paint to dry between coats.
Paint the whole box white. Our container began brilliant red and dark, so it took a couple of paint layers to cover totally.
Cover the whole box outside with sparkle paint.
Include a thick layer of Mod Podge to the highest point of the crate top. Quickly sprinkle sparkle, confections, and other little embellishments and sprinkles

over the Mod Podge. Leave a space in the middle so you can include the unicorn horn later. I likewise utilized a sparkly drop in certain regions. Get imaginative and all the little shimmers and glittery things you'd like; simply ensure they adhere to the Mod Podge.

Allow to dry completely - this may take a medium-term.

Make the unicorn horn with dirt. At that point, I make a cone shape, a long meager snake that I curved around the cone. Paint and include sparkle after it is heated.

Seal the top - we utilized a shower sealer. You could utilize Mod Podge, however, take care not to spread the shades of the sprinkles and confections.

Glue the horn to the principal focus of the top. We utilized heated glue. Customary specialty paste would likewise work extraordinary, and we simply aren't sufficiently quiet to sit tight for dry time.

Optional - utilizing a silver Sharpie marker or paint, add a dozing unicorn face to the front of your container.

SUNFLOWER CUPCAKE TOPPERS

MATERIALS

Cricut machine and Cricut Design Space
Flower
White cardstock
Printer
Glue
Toothpick

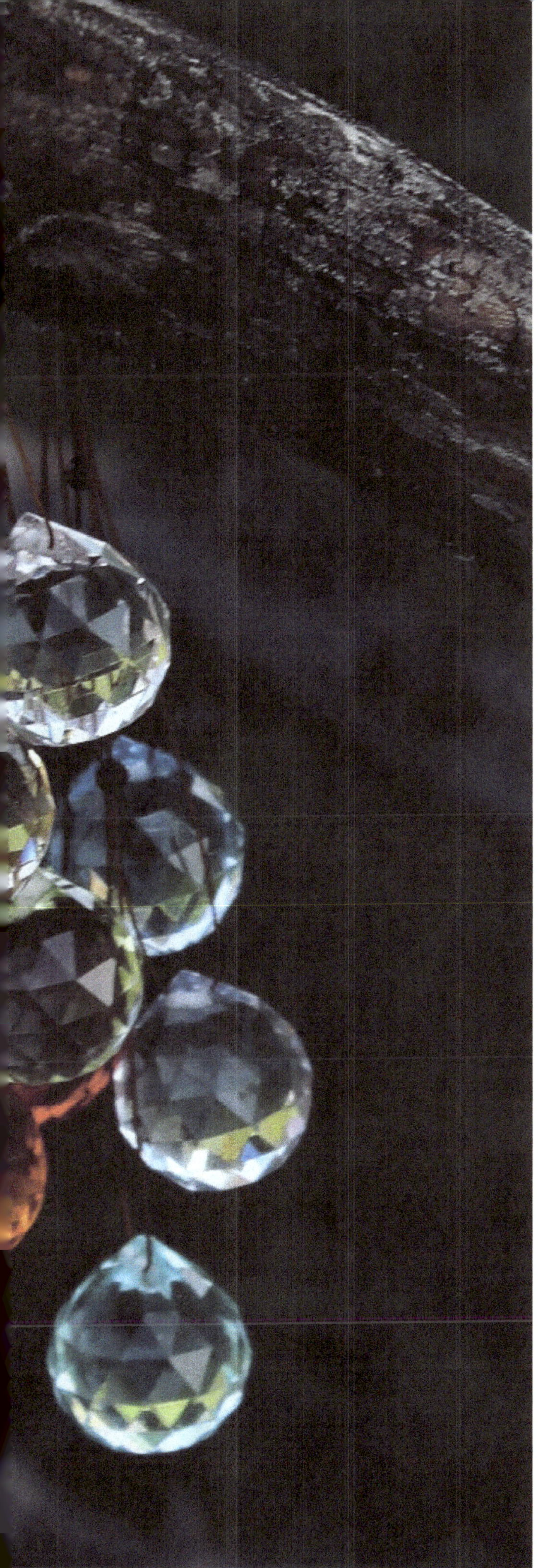

DIRECTIONS

Go to the preset Cricut project canvas and adhere to on-screen directions to print and cut each structure piece. Before cutting, try to quantify your structure and apply any estimating changes for the cupcakes you are utilizing before cutting.

Glue a toothpick on the rear of each blossom stem, leaving about 1" of toothpick at the base.

Place the toothpick into the highest point of the cupcake.

Alternatively, you can add a pretty cupcake wrapper to every cupcake. I like to prepare the cupcakes in a standard heating cup and afterward enhance them with a vivid wrapper. I've incorporated a pretty bloom cupcake wrapper right now for you to modify if you'd like.

EASY SUN CATCHERS WITH COLORING PAGES

MATERIALS NEEDED

Colored craftsmanship page or shading page - imprinted on essential white printer paper

Mason container covers (Wide Mouth Mason Jar Bands)

Oil - I utilized olive oil. However, any sort of oil should work.

Cotton balls

Scissors

Twine

Glue - (I utilize Aleene's Tacky Glue)
Paper towel - to secure work region and retain abundance oil
Easy Sun Catcher supplies

DIRECTIONS

Use cotton to apply oil to your specialty. Make a point to cover all the paper. You don't need to douse the paper, simply spread it. Touch overabundance oil up with a paper towel or tissue and permit to dry for around 5 minutes.

Using the bricklayer container cover, follow a hover around the craft and cut the hover inside the line so the craftsmanship fits inside the artisan top.

Apply a tad of paste inside the top and spot the craftsmanship in the cover, artistry side confronting outward.

Wrap twine around the top, attach a bunch to hold set up. Leave at any rate 4″ of twine and tie a bunch at the top so you can hang your suncatcher. That's it!

FELT CHRISTMAS TREE AND DECORATIONS

MATERIALS NEEDED

(Optional-to render a tree template) Wrapping paper or newspaper

Two sheets per color should be appropriate for numerous other felt sheet colors (blue, brown, yellow, white, orange, red, black, etc.).

1 Yard Green felt (for tree making)

Free Cricut Connection in Cricut Design Space to

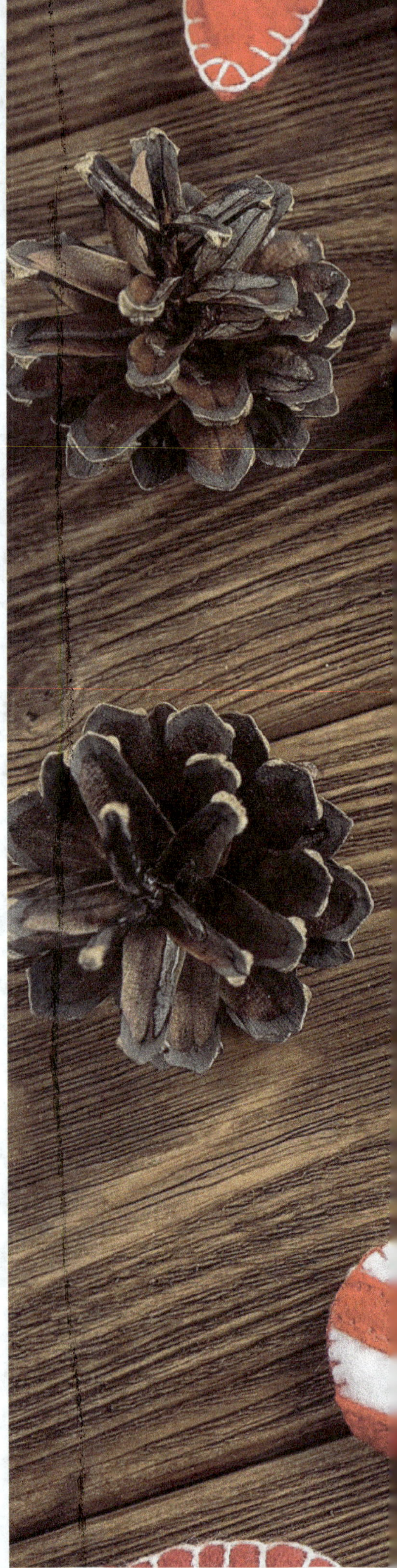

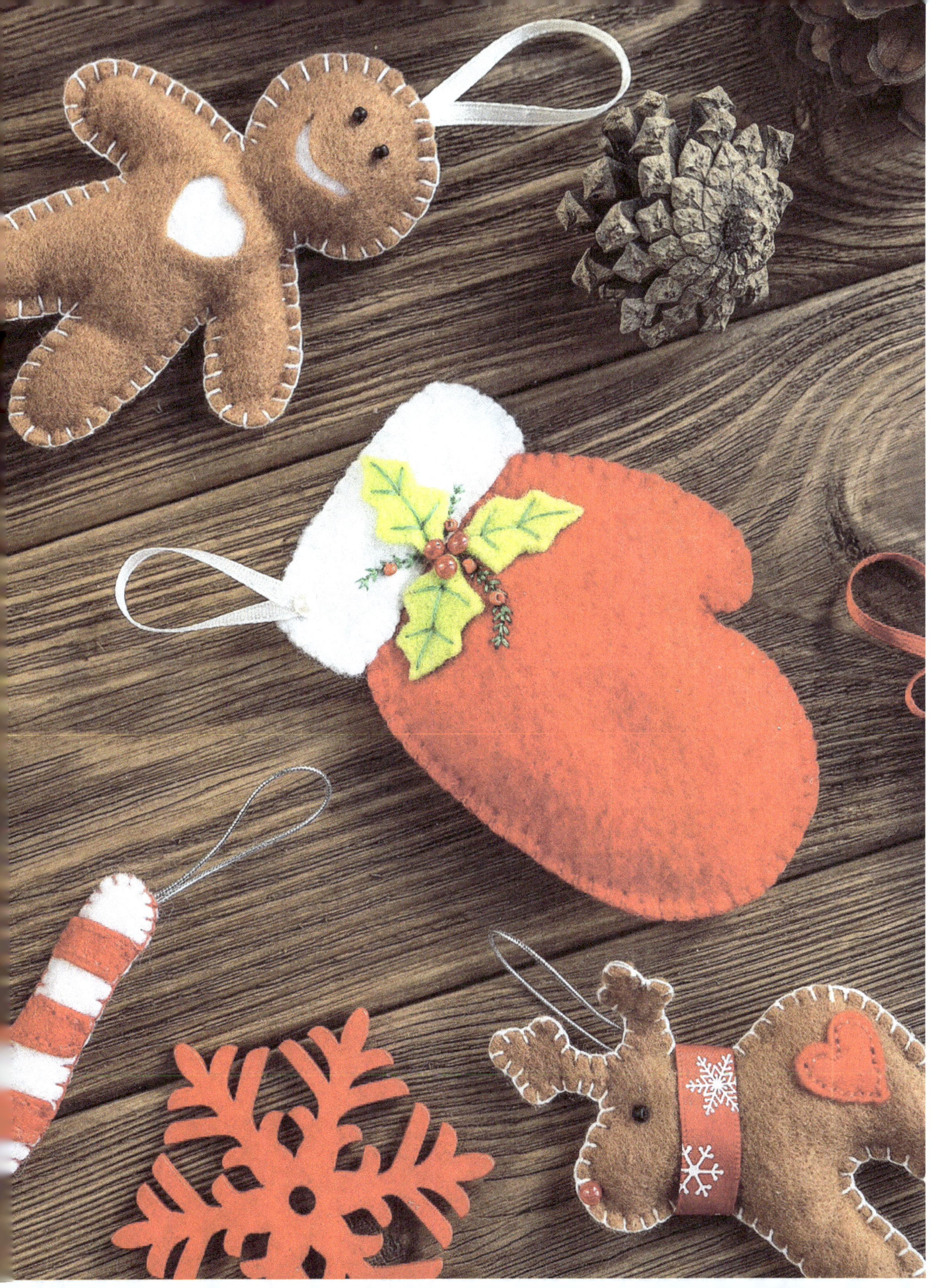

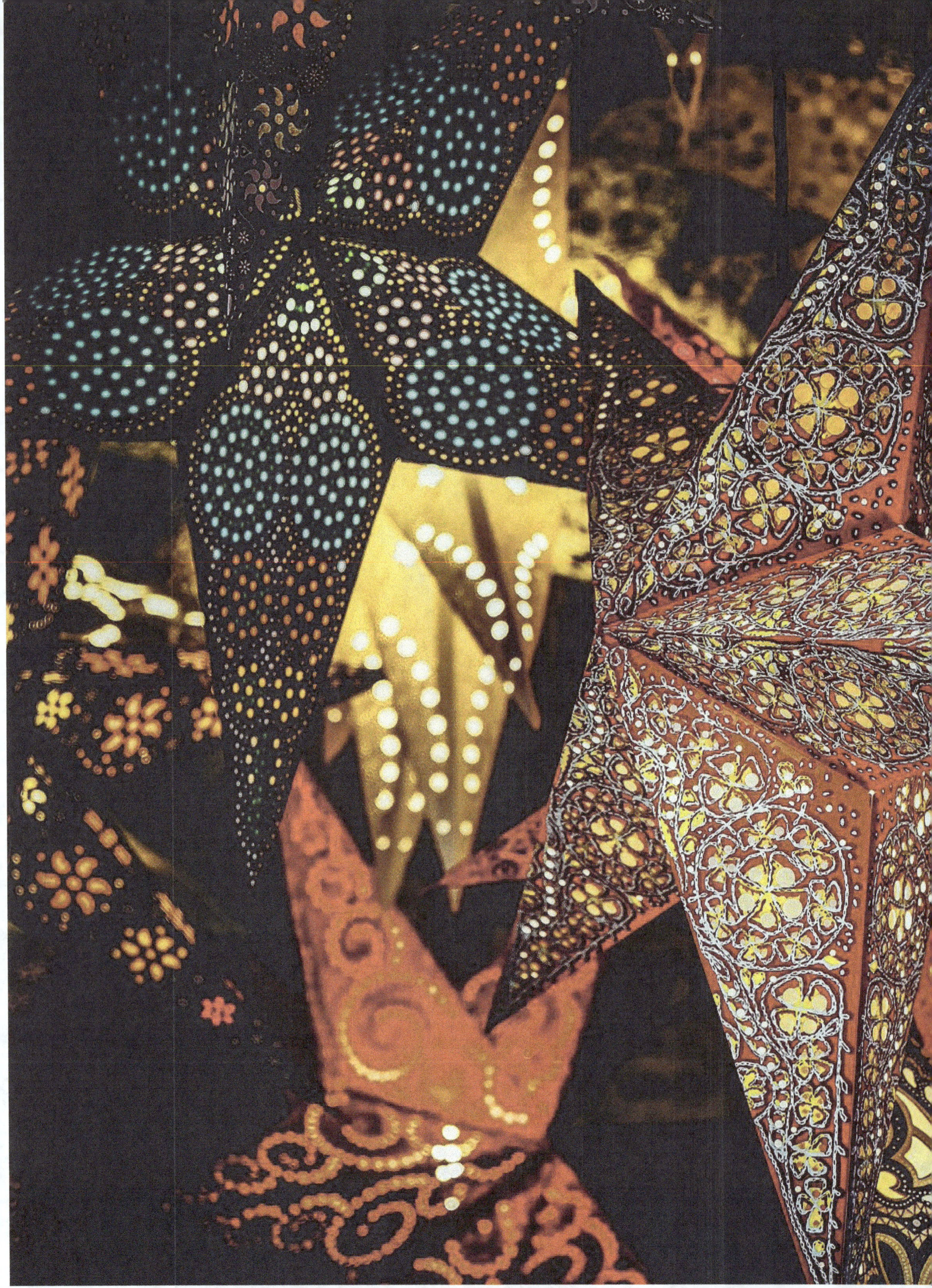

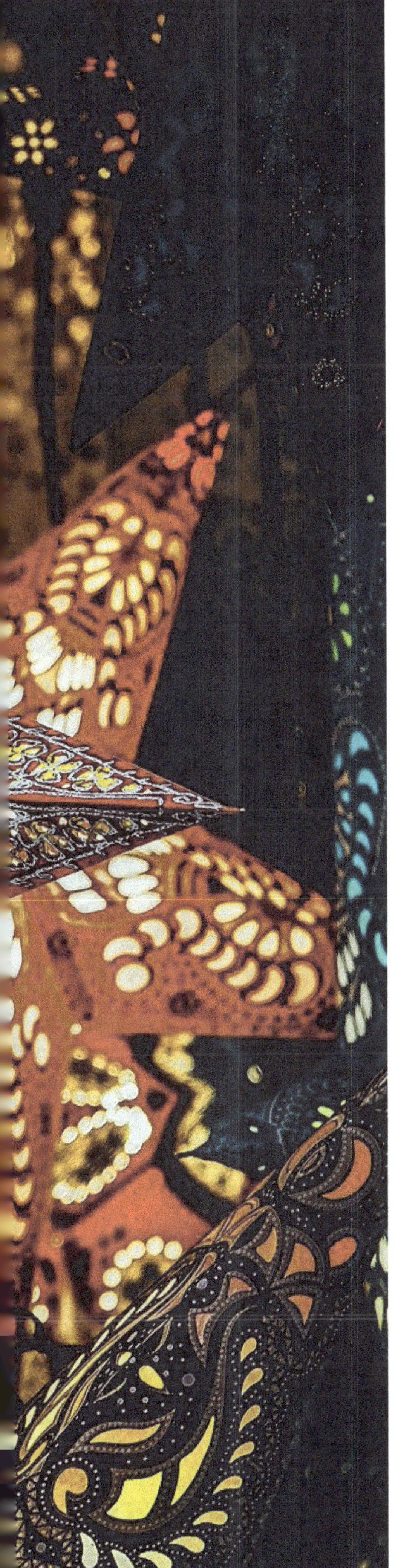

render it now (get it in my private library)
(To tie the tree to the wall) Green masking tape
Cricut Creator Machine (for this, you might also use Cricut Explore or Air, but FYI, I used the Creator Machine)

DIRECTIONS

Cut a broad tree outline utilizing the wrapping paper or newspaper. First, I took this measure to ensure that my tree came out the way I expected without messing up the feeling. To shape a tree, you should also cut out four small triangles.
Using the template to remove the tree-shaped green felt. Cut the ornaments from the felt
Glue the layers of ornament along (if required).
Let the little ones play with their new tree for fun! When not in usage, you should even create a little pocket to carry the ornaments.

CREATING 3-D CHRISTMAS LIGHTS

MATERIALS NEEDED

Various shades of felt (I used blue, black, purple, orange, green, and red)
Thread in color matching
Printable prototype for free
Computer to Cricut Builder (optional)
Device for Sewing
Stuffing (will perform cushion stuffing or batting)

DIRECTION

Break the light forms for Christmas. You have to have a left, a back, and a tip.

To the top of each lamp, stitch the black bits.

To make one long "ribbon," cut strips of black felt and tie the ends together.

Sew together the bottom of the bulbs, then the stuff.

Through the gap at the top of each lamp, string the black felt "ribbon" to build your garland.

Stitch the top of the closed lights and "ribbon" to the black felt. Suspend it on the tree and love it.

You can render as long or as short as you want your felt Xmas tree garland. I made two in each hue, and I made a wreath large enough just to hang over a lamp or a tiny flower.

CHRISTMAS ORNAMENTS

MATERIALS NEEDED

Cricut Machine
Clear Plastic Ornamentation
White Craft Paint (for better performance, suggest this brand in Wedding Cake color)
Ribbon
Vinyl Decals
Transfer tape
Weeder
Scrapper

DIRECTION

Cover the decorations with white paint and tap softly before white paint is covered on the bottom.

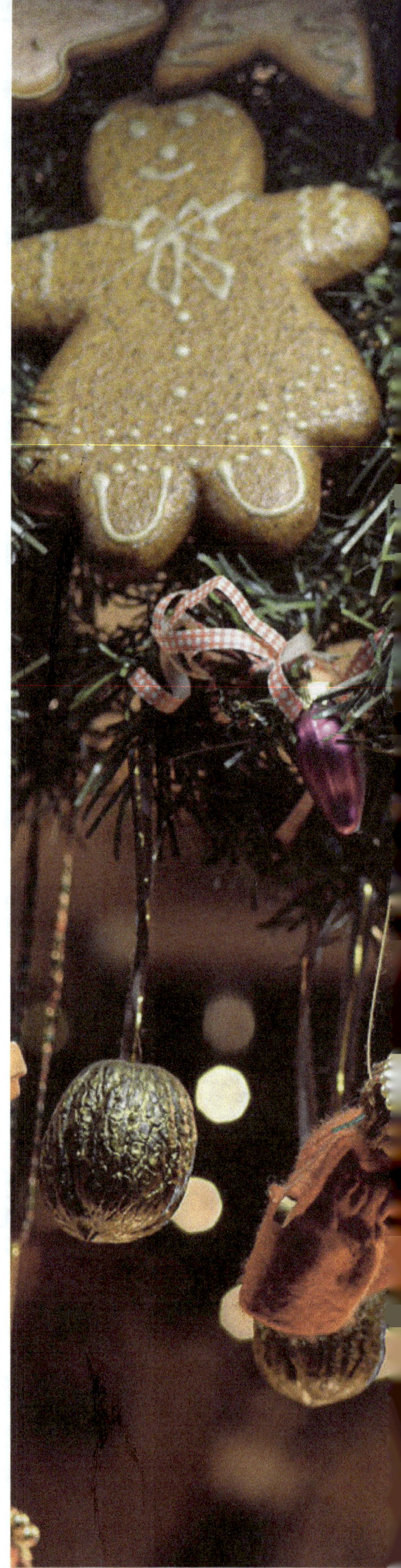

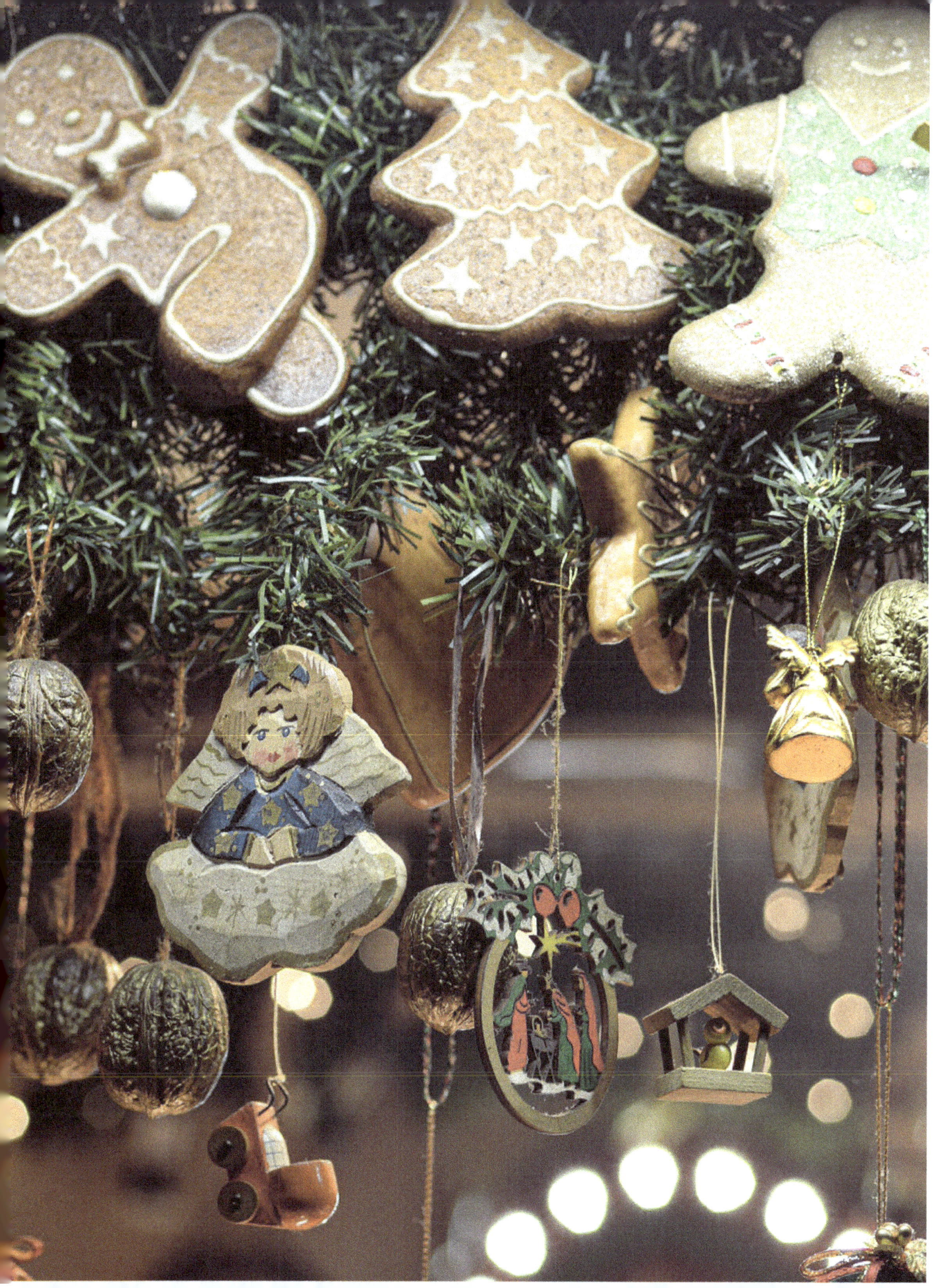

Don't pour too much ornament paint inside! When creating these ornaments, this is the dilemma I've learned most people have. Within, they place way too much color, and so it spills or never dries. If you think you put so much pain inside, switch the ornaments over and let them drip out until there is no stripping paint inside on a safe surface.
Replace the top of the ornament with the rear.
If you have purchased the decals from my store, build and cut the Cricut Images or skip this step.
Weed the vinyl off and apply the design.
Apply Ribbon, and it's ready.

CHRISTMAS VILLAGE PAPER ORNAMENTS

MATERIALS NEEDED

Low-temp hot glue handgun
Tool for burnishing
Vinyl cutting-machine
Weeding method
Thread with gold embroidery
Material from vinyl transition
Scissors
White card inventory report

DIRECTIONS

Break the scene of your village from white card stock.
Fold all score lines up.
Glue tabs and scenario bits are added.
To involve cliffs, higher towers, and lower towers, connect three levels. Ensure that all folds display a

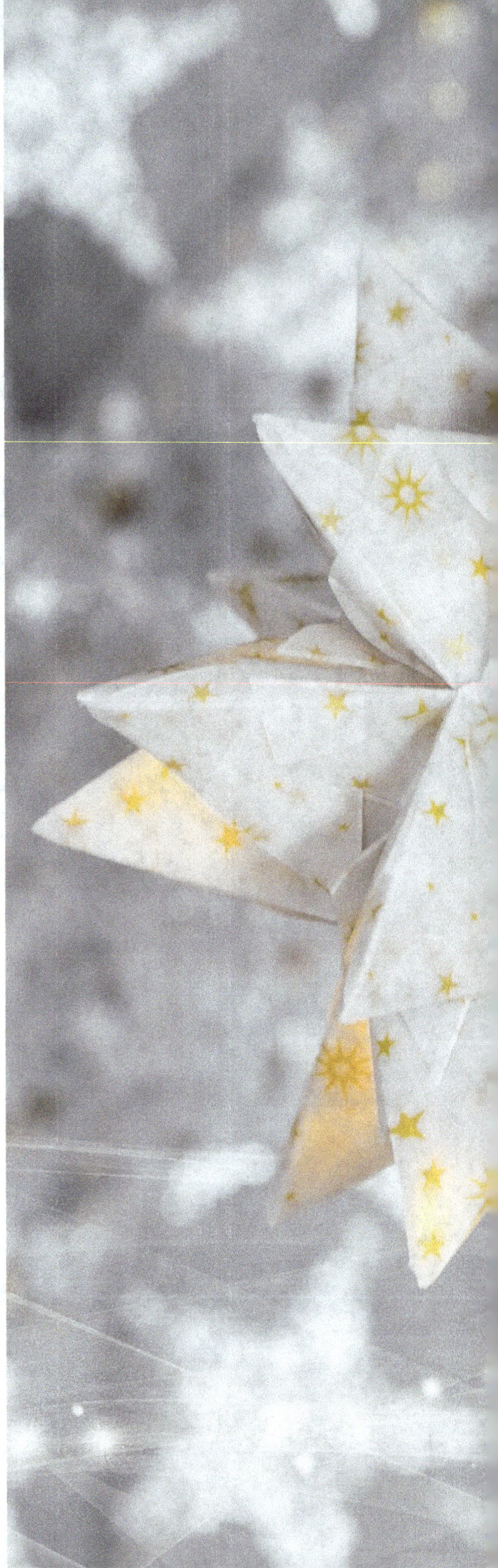

zigzag that is compatible with all three layers. For a tiny home, cut from a stock of white cards.

Fold all score lines up.

Glue the tab on the house's side and click to lock it.

For a mini-lantern, glue the rooftop within the building.

Glue the top tabs outward for adornment. Loop string gold embroidery through the hole to hang on the tree.

They're happy to add decorations to your buildings or put on a limb.

MINI WREATHS FOR THE PARTY

MATERIALS NEEDED

Pliers with needle-nose and wire cutters
Broad green ribbon, perfect for giant wreaths
Curling tool for Paper
Curling tool for Paper
Slender ribbon for a mini wreath
Hot glue gun low-temp
Form of the wreath
Floral wire-wrapped brown paper

DIRECTIONS:

Shape a mini wreath by wrapping floral wire filled with brown paper into a loop. To form your bits of conifer, fir, and dawn redwood, take measures from a wide wreath.

Glue coppice needles, slightly contrasting parts,

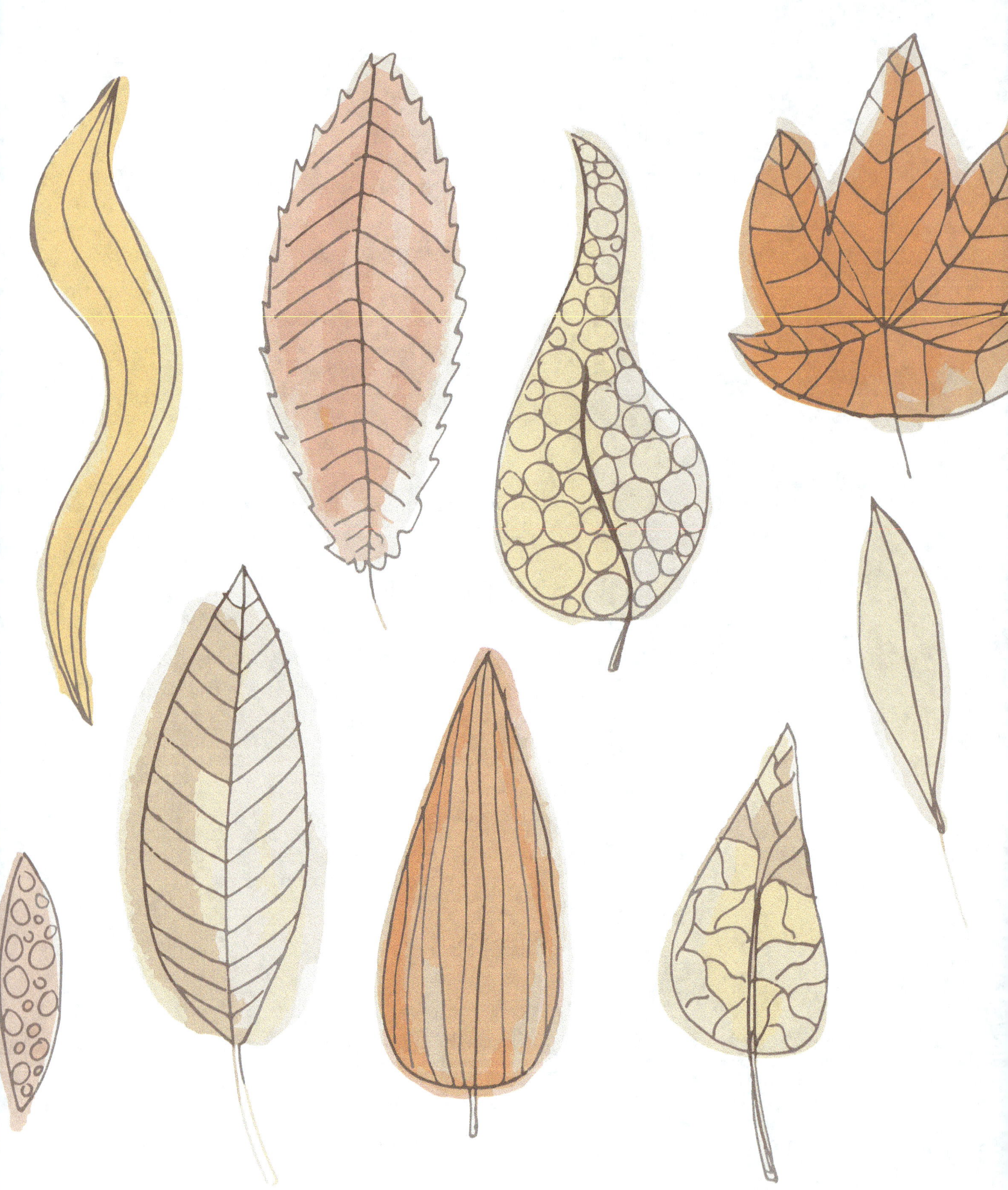

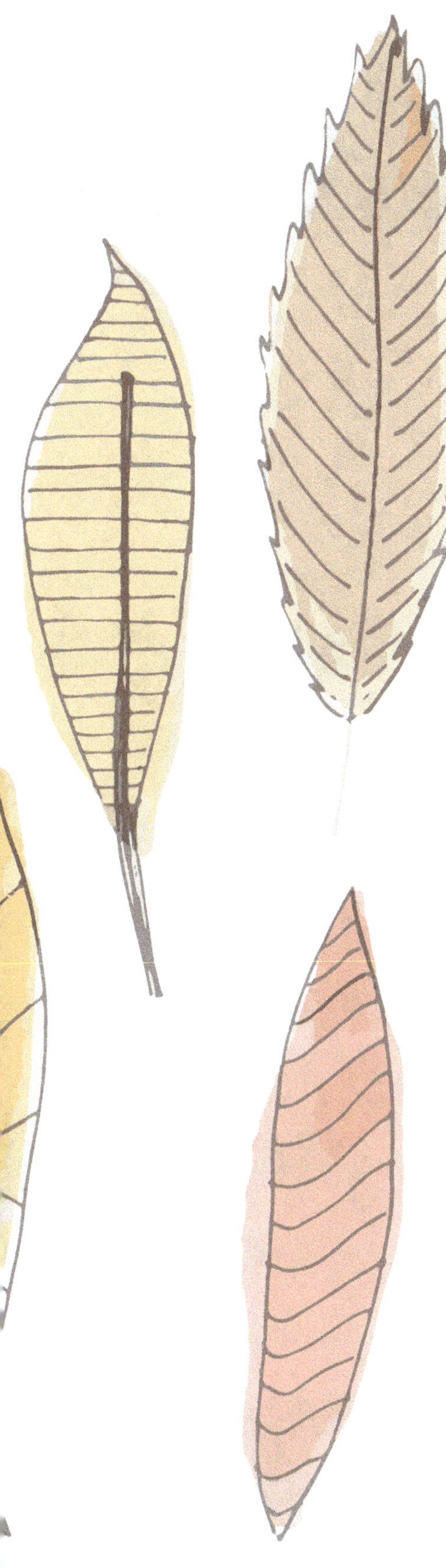

onto the wire wreath.

Glue fir needles to slightly conflicting bits on the wire wreath.

Glue boxwood leaf, partially contrasting parts, on a wire wreath.

Loop ribbon via rope, double knot tie.

Slide the knot to meet the wire and apply a drop of safe adhesive.

MAKING FALL FOLIAGE

MATERIALS NEEDED

Card Inventory Documents
Computer by Cricut Cutting
Wreath of Grape Vine (for broad wreath)
Vellum or vellum
Paint and brush for crafts (optional)
Curling tool for document
Hot glue gun low-temp
Text frosted-weight weight
7-inch (for mini wreaths) gold hoops

DIRECTIONS

Break and rate the card paper, carbon paper, or text-weight leaves.

Leaves fold into score lines.

For forming leaves, use a curling tool.

Start with the folding middle scoreline for leaves with several scores.

To form the mat, push the curling tool into the score lines.

Glue leaf in combination onto grapevine type to

create broad wreaths.

Glue leaves spin on the metal hoop for mini wreaths.

Brush tones of color onto paper for the painted leaves. Before forming and folding, let dry.

Tip: We cut forms from craft paper for our colored foliage and applied the color with paint. In the finished look, gold or other shiny finishes give a stunning sheen and texture.

MERRY CHRISTMAS IN DIFFERENT LANGUAGES

MATERIALS NEEDED

8" x 10" timber Plaque
White Vinyl Adhesive
Maker Cricut
Tools Cricut (optional)
Tape Transfer
Paintbrush Paints
The Mat
Paint (I used Acrylic Christmas Red by Deco Art Crafter)
Space File for Christmas Sign Template (if you like to use mine)

DIRECTIONS:

You need to use different fonts to write different greetings and merry Christmas signs in different languages.

Then paint the board and put it aside to dry when your template is cut out.

Please ensure your vinyl machine is ready, attach

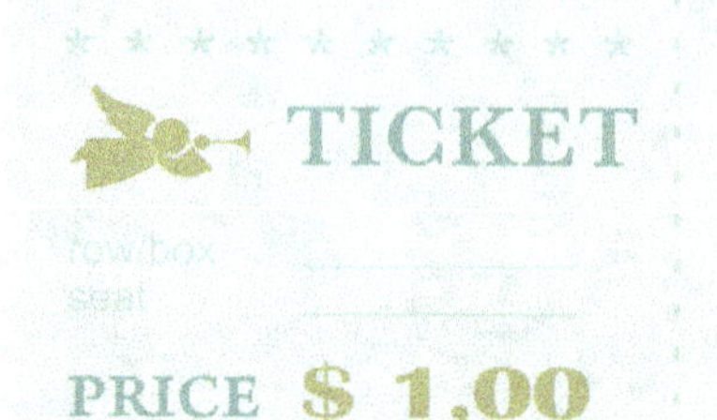

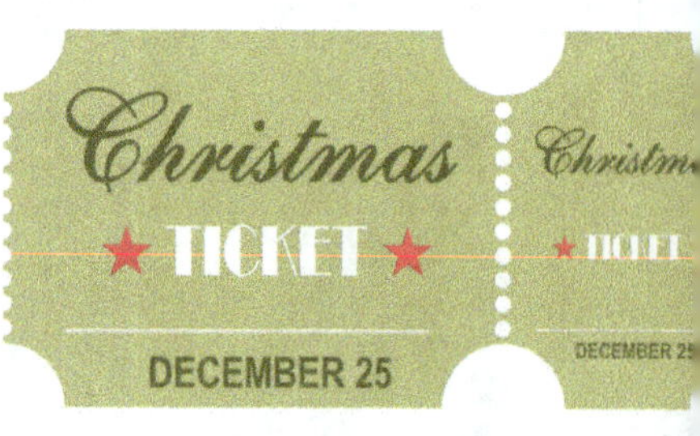

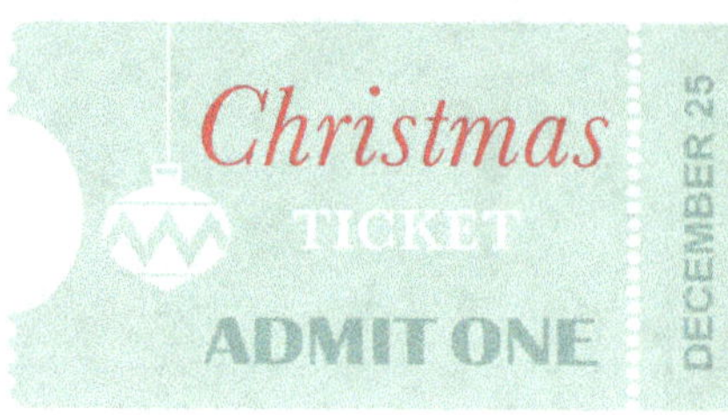

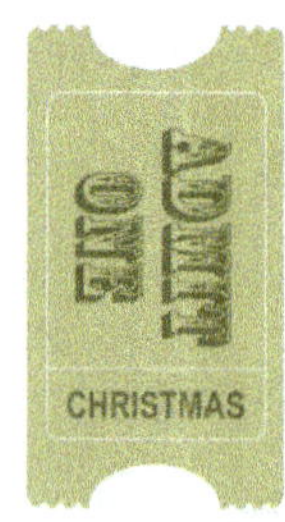

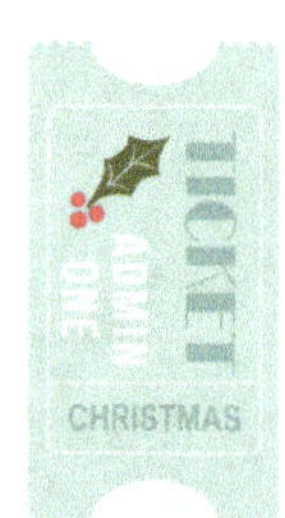

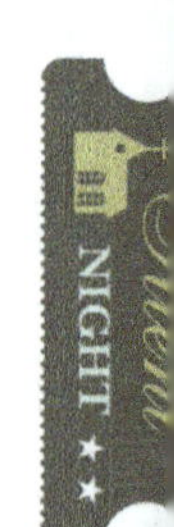

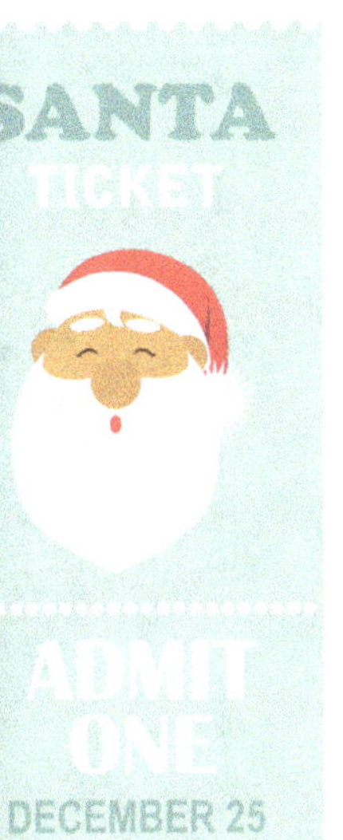

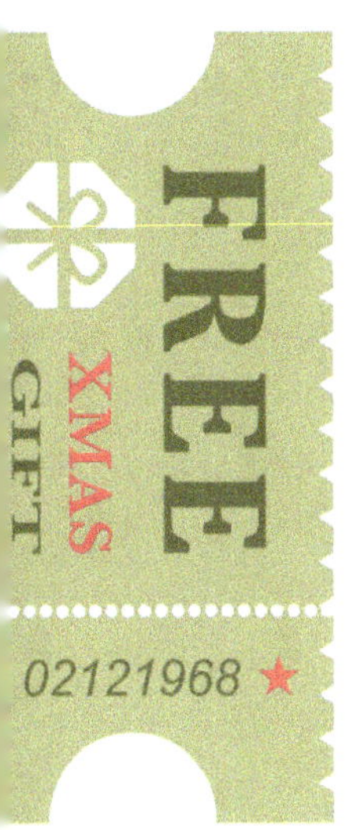

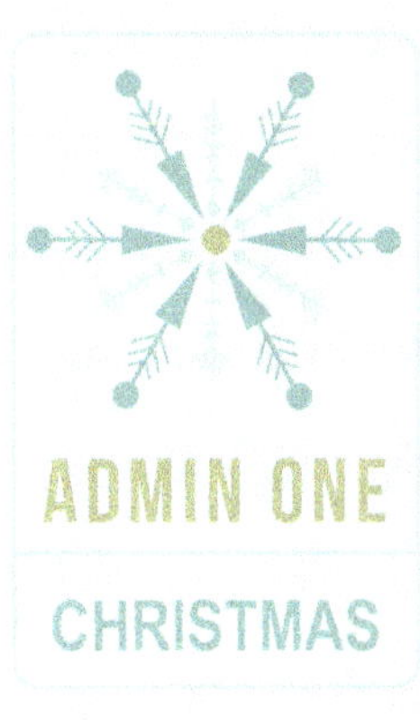

your vinyl to the mat, load it into the machine, and cut it.

Break the strip of vinyl and weed it out. Then gently take off the backing, stick the transfer tape on. Please hold to the board and strip the transfer tape off.

Chapter 5
Valentine's Day

VALENTINE'S DAY PILLOW

MATERIALS NEEDED:

Explore Air 2 by Cricut
Red Shimmer Iron-on Vinyl
Cover for Pillow
12 x 24 Board Cricut
Tools Cricut
Board with Iron **&** Ironing

DIRECTION

To begin with, you're going to want to find a picture, create your own, and you can use mine to find it here. In Cricut Design Room, read the directions here on how to download your file. You're able to cut once you have the file imported. At the top of your computer, press 'GO.' It'll get you to this link. You want to press the checkmark on 'Reflection Picture (FOR IRON-ON)' as you cut the Iron-on.
Switch to the right spot on the dial, and you're ready to carve. As I cut iron-on vinyl glitter, I want to place the dial on the setting of Iron-on +.
Place the iron-on vinyl on your mat, shiny side down, then trim the print.
When removed, use the weeding method to bring

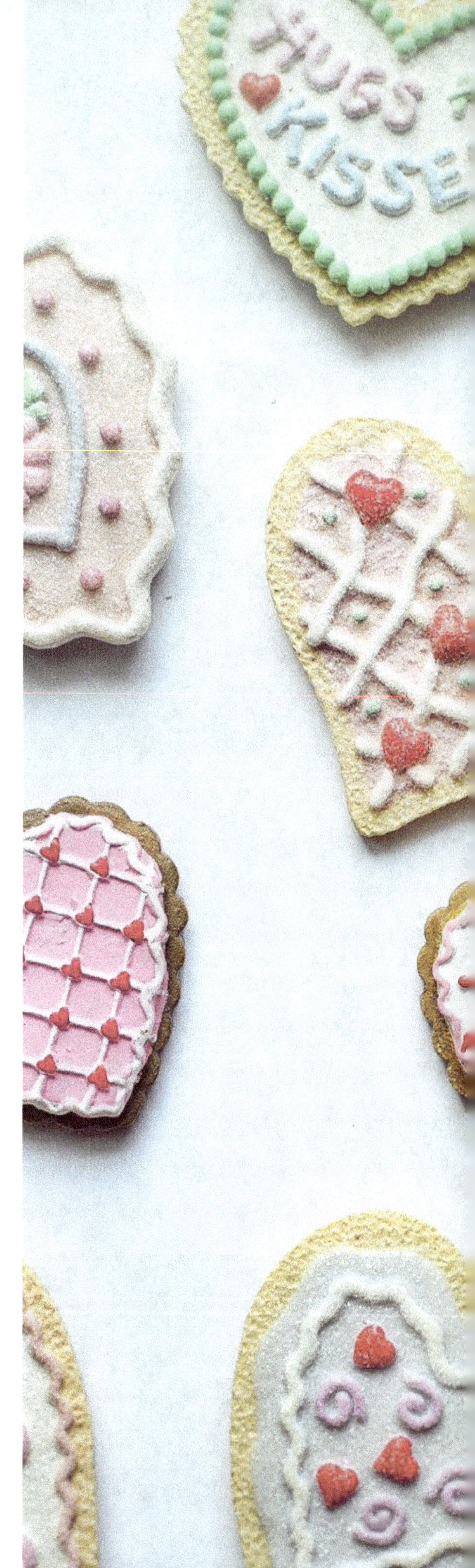

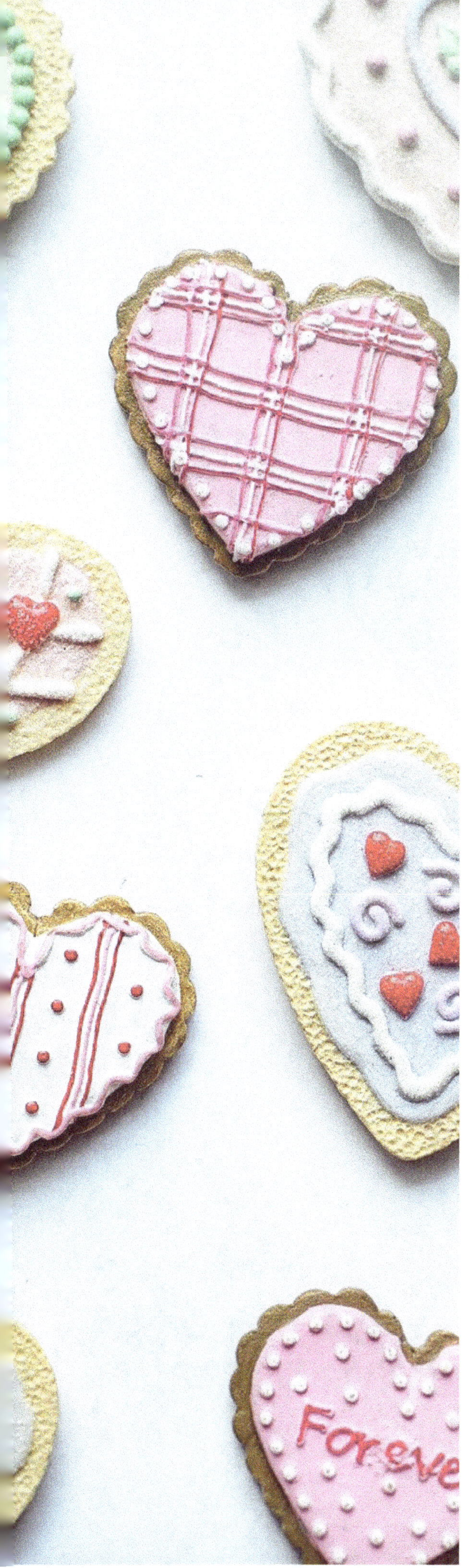

all the negative vinyl out.

On the ironing board, put your pillow cover and steam it up with your iron.

On the pillow, put your cutaway iron-on vinyl portrait.

Place a towel over the top of the image and iron it. Making sure you iron all over the photo long enough, or if you have a soldering iron, that works much better.

Peel the plastic mask off until the portrait has been sealed down to the pillowcase.

Using a pillow insert to fill your pillow cover and put it in your home anywhere you like it.

It is the ideal addition to every home for Valentine's Day, and this pillow will also be an excellent addition to the master bedroom.

HELLO DARLING CARD

MATERIALS NEEDED

Coordinating cardstock
Cricut scoring tool
Cricut machine
Pink and central paper pads
Glue dots or mini glue dots
Cricut light cutting mat grip

DIRECTION

Open the Design Space and start a new project. Click on the Images file to locate the one that you wish to use.

Insert that file into the project canvas.
Send this file to the Cricut machine, and then use the cut designated for cardstock using the light cutting mat.
Apply your glue dots onto the back of the cards inside.
Press the designer cardstock with the glue dots.
Repeat this process to create many more cards that will brighten your friends' and families' days.

CALFSKIN HAIR BOW

MATERIALS NEEDED

Cricut Investigate
Faux calfskin or cowhide
Transfer tape
Strong grasp Cricut tangle
Bow Cricut configuration space document
E6000 paste
French barrette clasps
Binding clasps

DIRECTION

Line your artificial softened cowhide or calfskin with your exchange tape. This will give something for the texture to clutch instead of leaving fluff everywhere on your tangle and nearly demolishing it. This was an immense help, and I will never return to staying the texture ideal on the concrete hold tangle

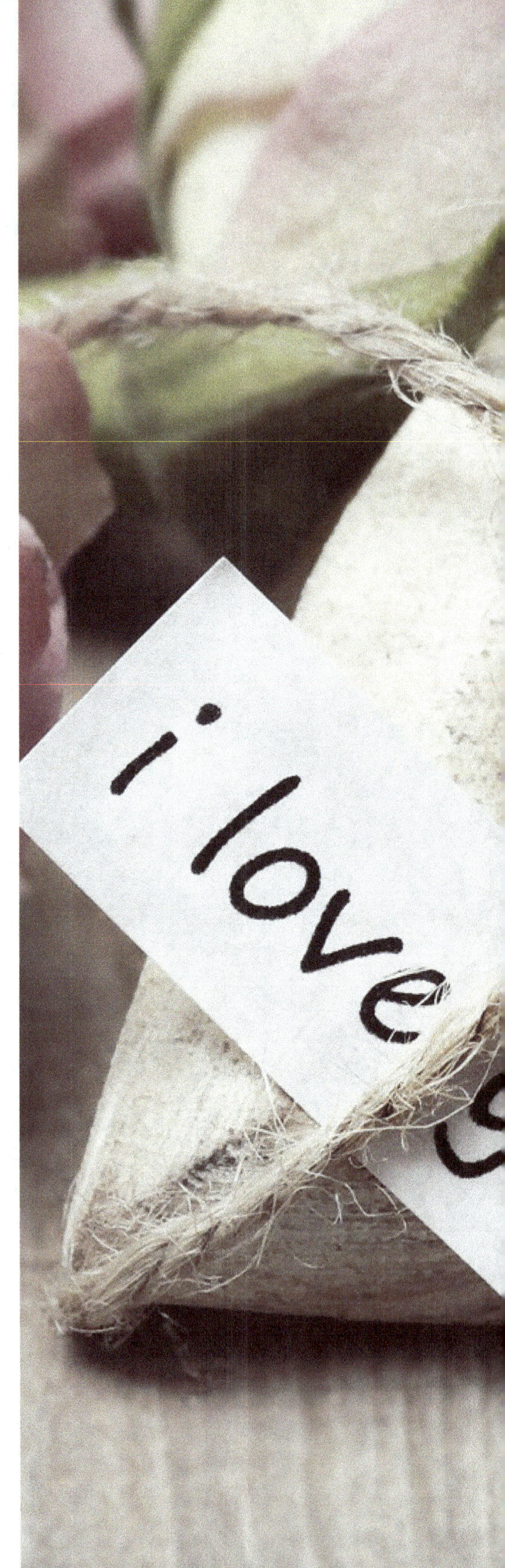

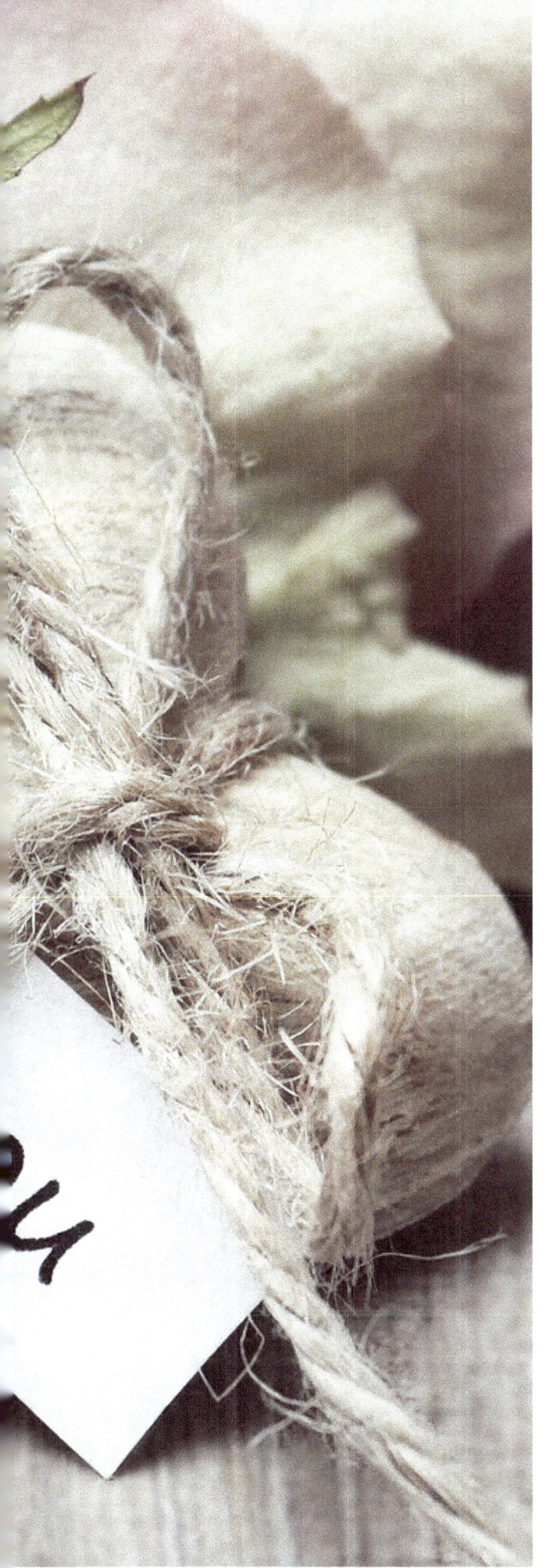

again.

When you pick the artificial cowhide setting on your Keen Dial, it will slice through the item twice. When your pictures are excessively near one another, occasionally, it will catch and draw the item. To stay away from this, move your pictures promote separation when you see your tangle. This will spare items over the long haul and spare a lot of cerebral pains. Try not to be hesitant to utilize some scissors if you have one nick in the calfskin. Begin with every one of your pieces laid out. You will need to overlay the most extended piece with the goal that the finishes compromise. Secure that with the E6000 stick and a coupling cut. On the off chance you have made above one bow, right now is an ideal opportunity to gather all the more drawn-out pieces.

Next, you will assume the back and position the E6000 stick in the center. Take your bow piece and hold it fast to that, safe with a coupling cut. Enable it to dry only a couple of minutes in the middle of each progression. Next, put some E6000 on the barrette and lay the back piece to it. Take your little centerpiece and apply the paste to that. Overlay it over the bow in the center and around the back of the barrette. Secure that with a coupling cut. I would permit these to dry for a couple of hours before you stick them in their hair to ensure they do not get any paste on them.

VALENTINE'S DAY CLASSROOM CARDS

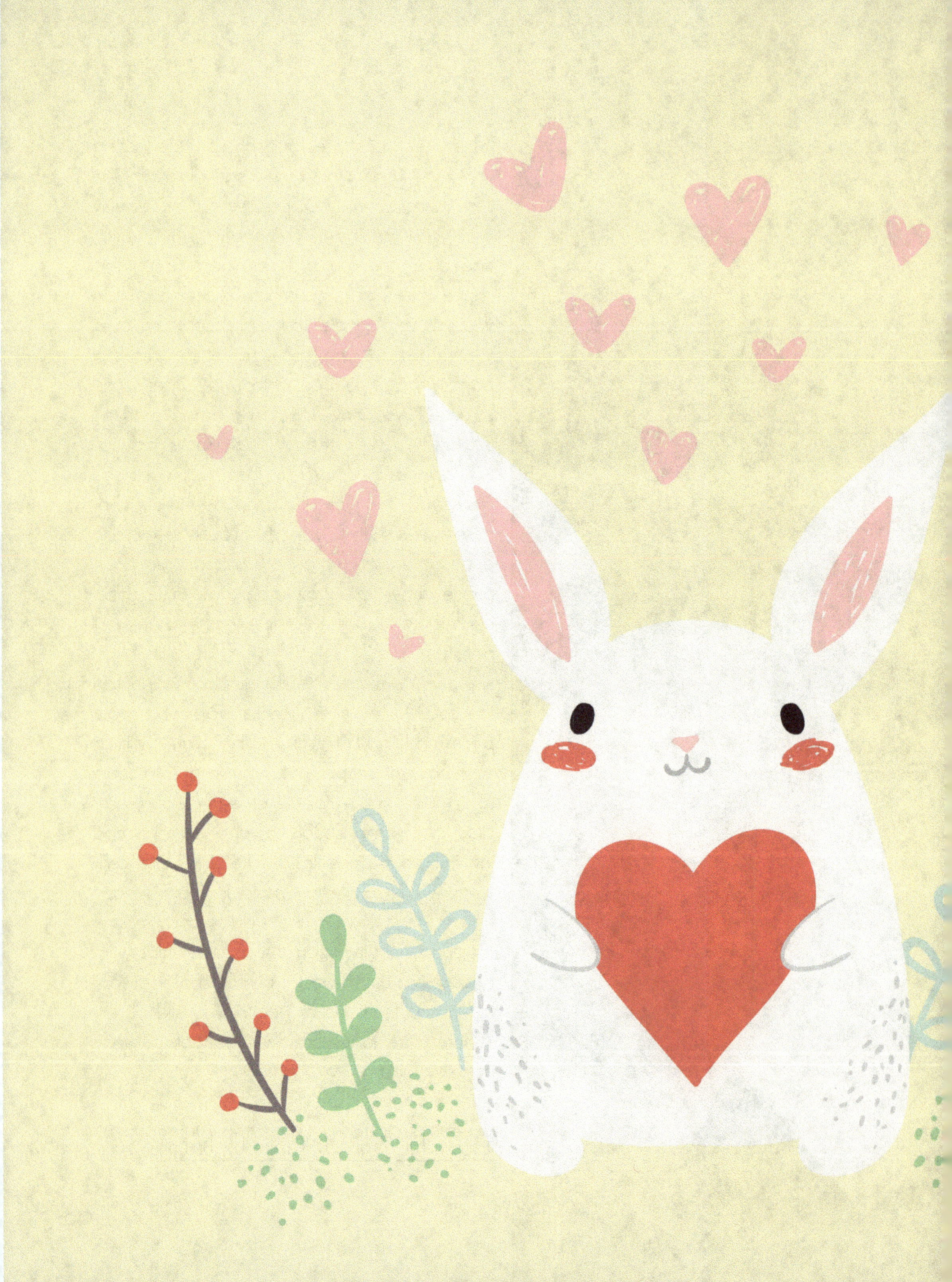

MATERIALS NEEDED:

Cricut Maker
Card Designs (Write Stuff Coloring)
Cricut Design Space
Dual Scoring Wheel
Pens
Cardstock
Crayons
Shimmer Paper

DIRECTION

Open the Card Designs (Write Stuff Coloring) on the Design Space, click on 'Make it' or 'Customize' to make edits.

When all the changes have been done, Cricut will request you to select a material. Select 'Cardstock' for the cards and 'Shimmer Paper' for the envelopes.

Cricut will send you a notification when you need to change the pen colors while creating the Card, and then it will start carving the Card out automatically.

You will be prompted later on to change the blade because of the Double Scoring Wheel. It is advisable to use the Double Scoring Wheel with Shimmer Paper; they both work best together.

When the scoring has been finished, replace the Scoring Wheel with the last blade.

After that, fold the flaps at the Score lines in the direction of the paper's white side, and then attach the 'Side Tabs' to the exterior of the 'Bottom Tab' by gluing them together.

You may now write 'From:' and 'To:' before placing the Crayons into the Slots.
Place the Cards inside the Envelopes and tag them with a sharp object.

PAPER LOLLIPOPS

MATERIALS NEEDED:

Cricut Maker, or Cricut Explore
Light grip mat
Patterned cardstock in desired colors
Glitter
Wooden Dowels
Hot Glue.

DIRECTION

Log into the 'Design Space' application and click on the 'New Project' button on the screen's top right corner to view a blank canvas.
Let us use an already existing project from the 'Cricut Library' and customize it. So click on the 'Projects' icon and type in 'Paper Lollipop' in the search bar.
Click on 'Customize' to edit the project to your preference further, click on the 'Make It' button, load the cardstock to your Cricut machine, and follow the Direction the screen to cut your project. Using hot glue, adhere the down between the lollipop circles. Brush them with craft glue and sprinkle them with glitter.

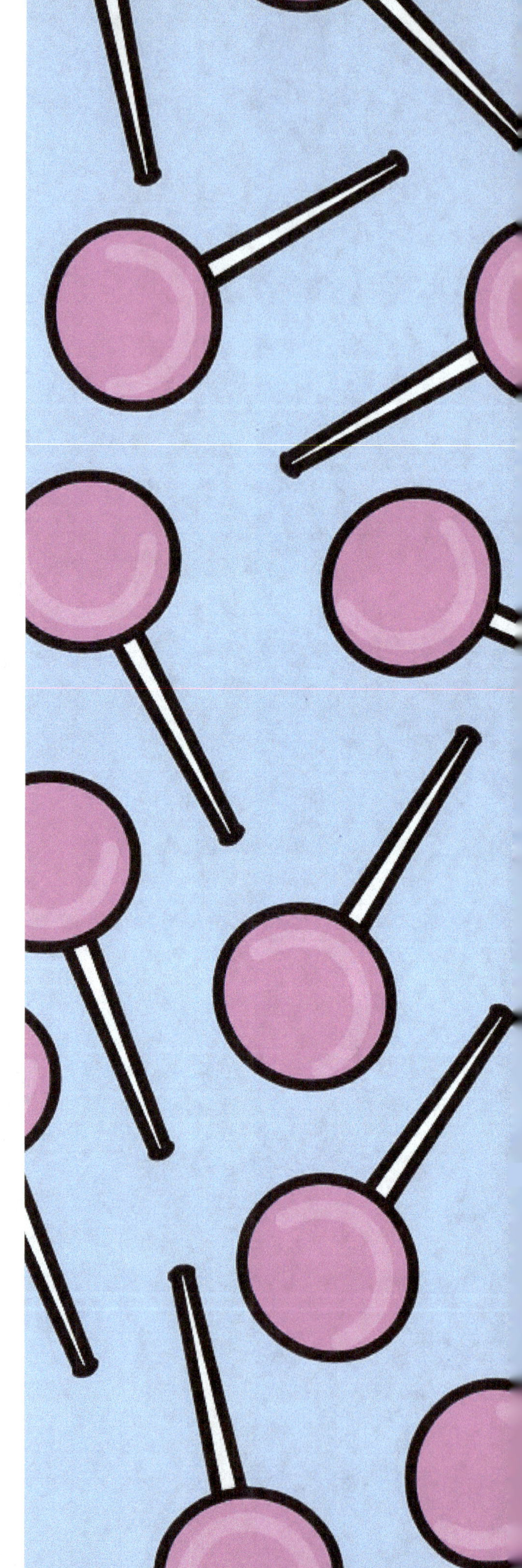

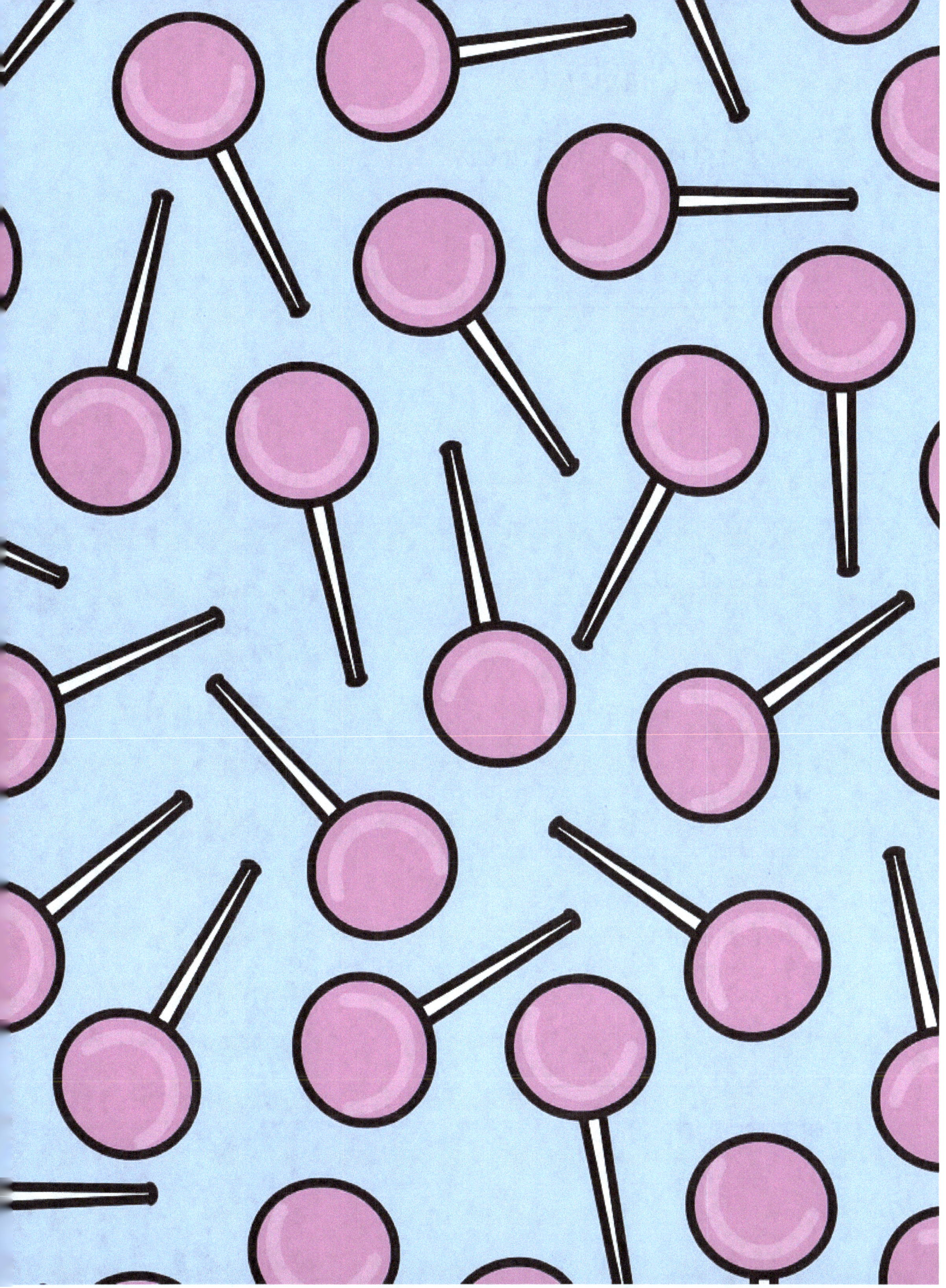

Chapter 6
Easter projects ideas

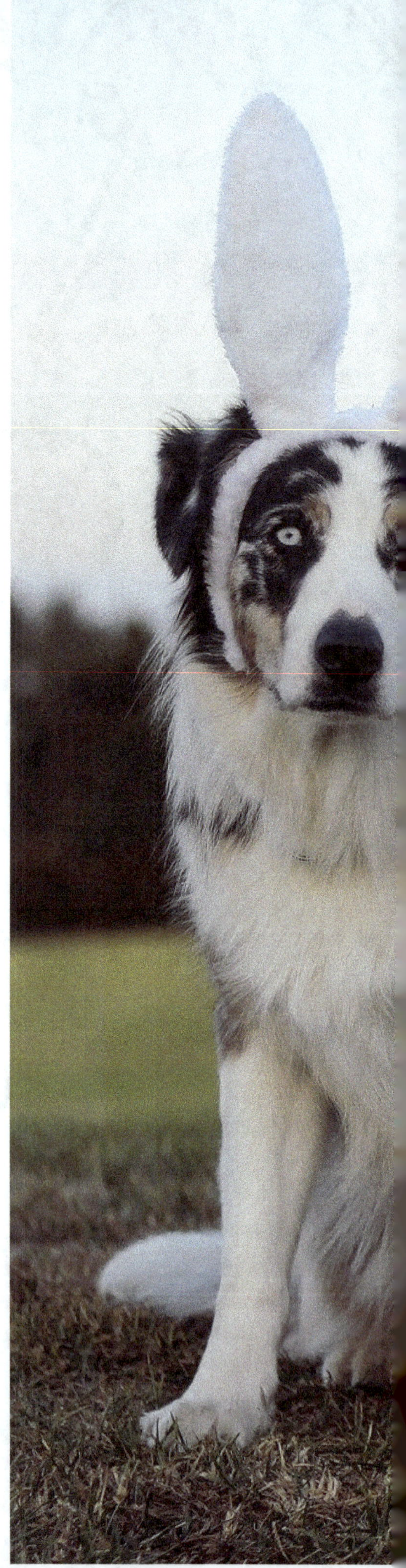

FAST EASTER BUNNY NAIL ART MATERIALS NEEDED

MATERIALS NEEDED

Nail clean
Quick-dry top coat - I incline toward Out the Door snappy dry top coat
Cricut Machine
Free Easter icons SVG cut record (see beneath)
Gold cement foil

DIRECTION

Paint your nails any way you'd like. I made an ombre look.
Upload the Easter icons SVG to Cricut Design Space.
Conceal all the icons aside from the rabbit body.
Therapist the rabbit picture to just shy of 1/4" wide.
Cut the picture utilizing the vinyl setting and gold glue foil.
Apply the rabbit cut out to your dry, painted nails.
Apply 2-3 layers of top coat to your nail, permitting the clean to dry between applications.

PRINTABLE EASTER EGG GARLAND

MATERIALS YOU NEED:

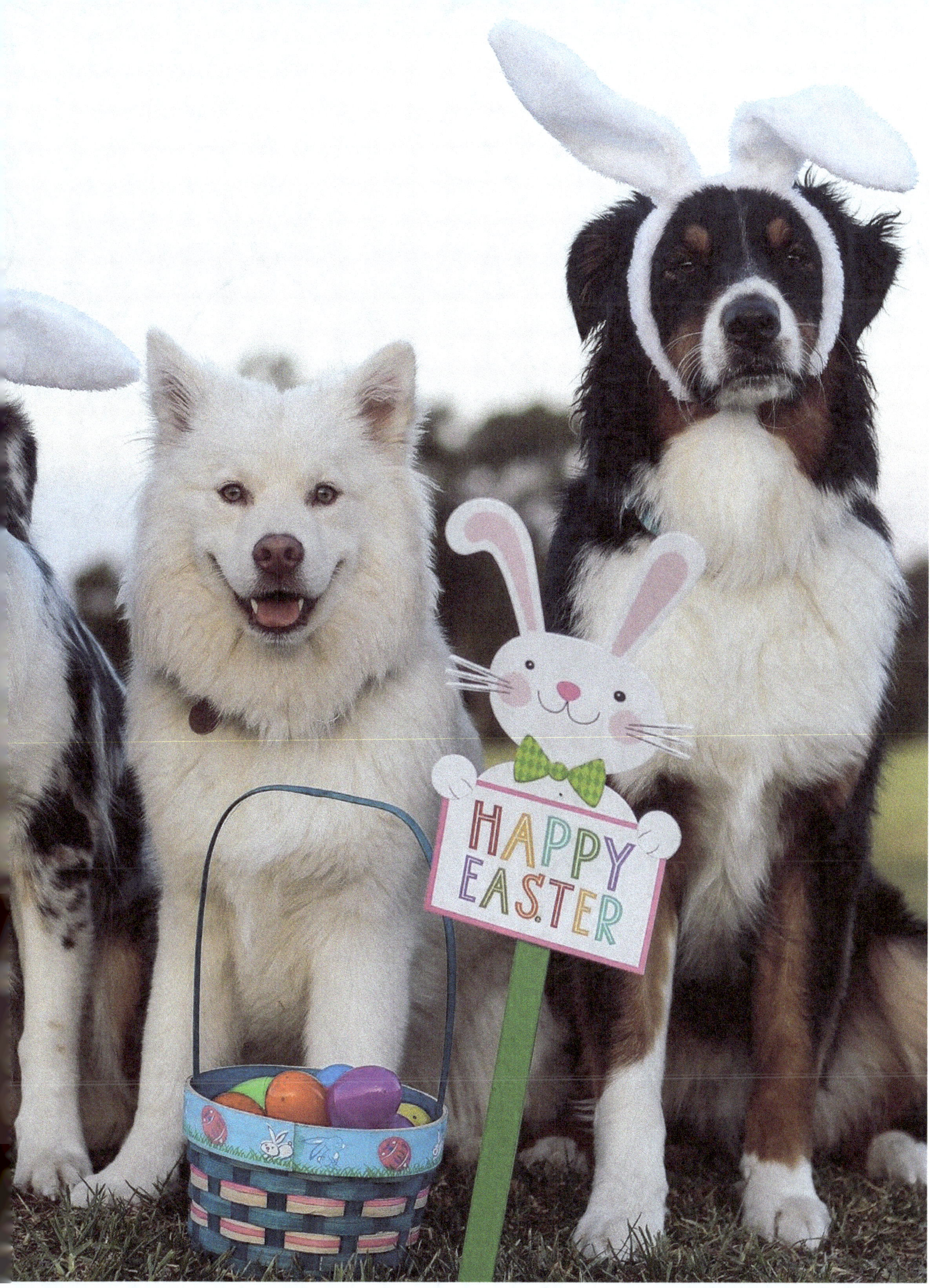

HAPPY
EASTER

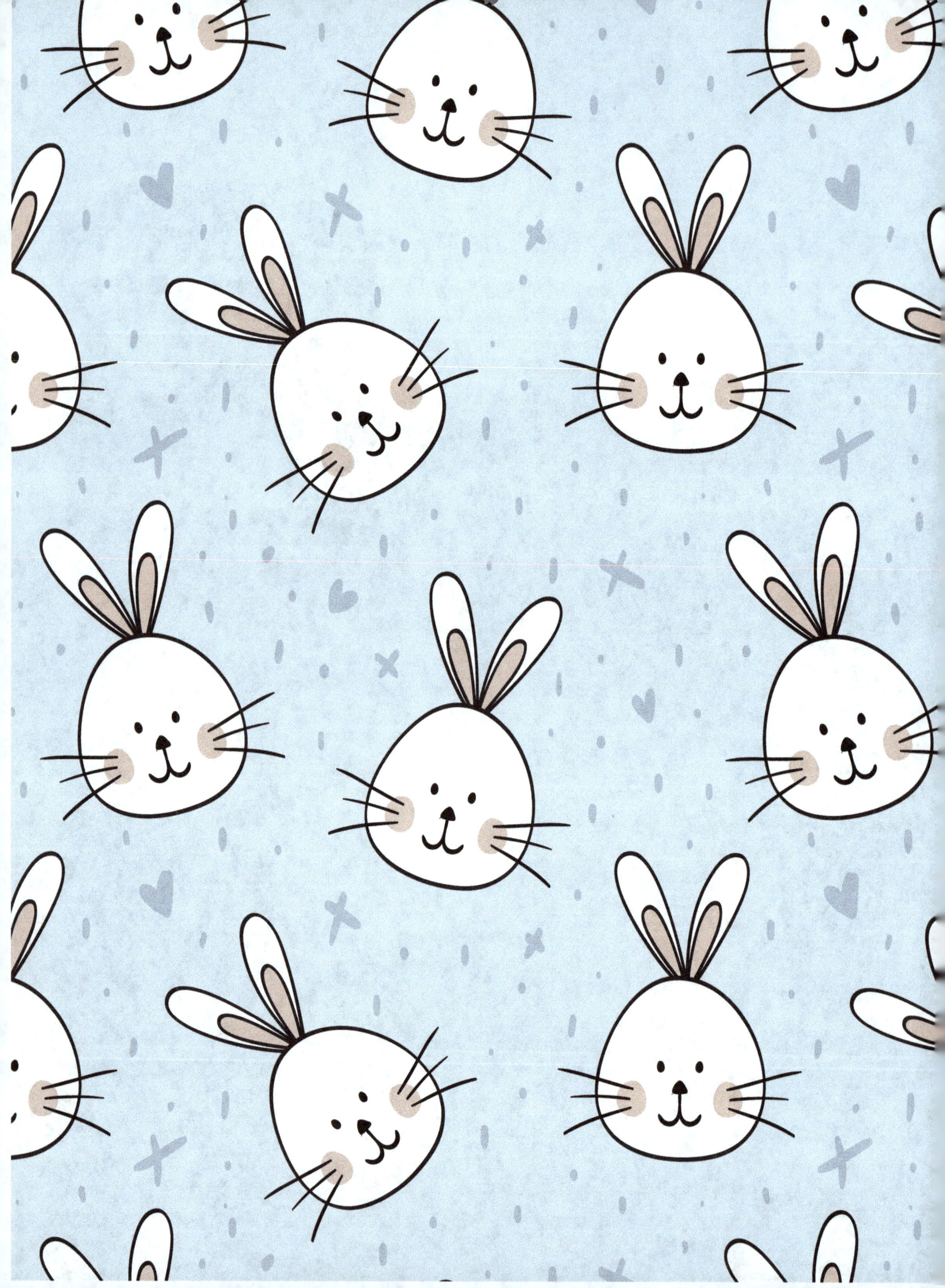

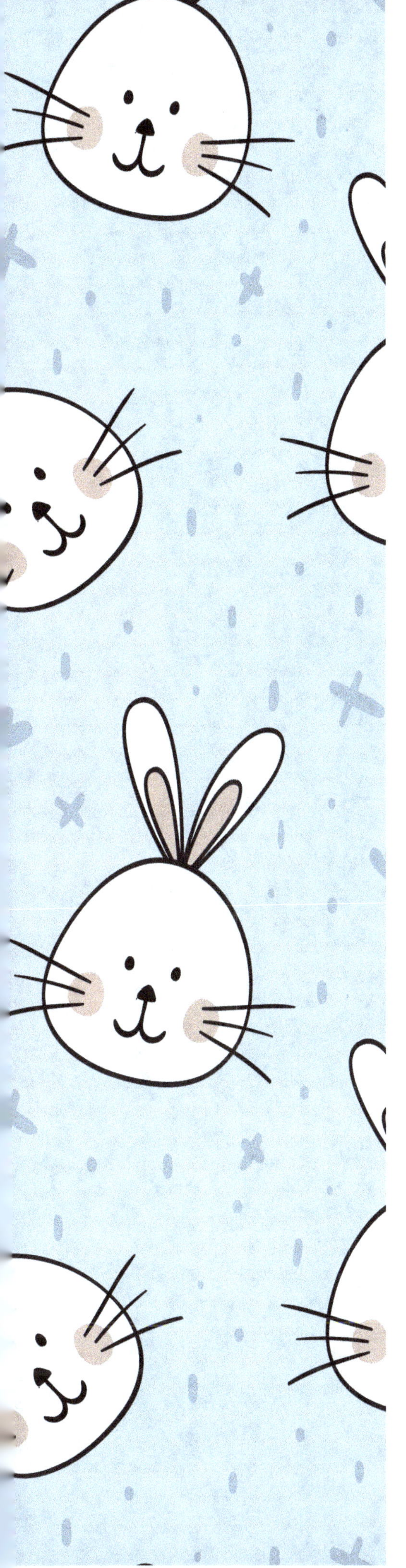

String
Hole punch
White card stock
Cutting machine or Scissor

DIRECTION

You can do this project either with a cutting machine or without. You can likewise set the project up to include a pretty draw line on the off chance that you have a Cricut Explore or a Cricut Air. This is an extraordinary tool to have the option to make a ton of these cute little paper Easter eggs before long!
In case you're utilizing a Cricut:
Go to Design Space
Upload the PNG record. Pick "Fundamental Upload" and afterward select "Complex Image." You shouldn't have to alter anything.
Upload the draw SVG record. Pick "Vector Upload."
Once the two records are uploaded to your structure library, you can choose them and add them to your Design Space configuration screen.
Make sure the drawing layer is the topmost layer and pick "compose." Join the two layers together. You ought to have the option to build the pictures' size to pretty much 7" vertically for the Print Then Cut page size cutoff points.
Follow the on-screen directions to print, draw, and cut the art design.
Use the gap punch to make an opening at the highest point of each egg. String together any way you'd like. Tie a little bunch at the highest point of each egg so they would lay level when you hang the laurel.

PLASTIC SPOON CHICKS FOR EASTER

MATERIALS NEEDED

Five plastic spoons
Five earthenware pots
Fine coarseness sandpaper
Pencil with a new eraser
Floral froth
Cardstock
White strip
White tissue paper
Hot stick weapon
White create stick
Craftsman paint:
Butter Cream-like DecoArt's Buttercream
Pink-like this Pink Chiffon
Grape Taffy
Pool Blue-marginally lighter in shading is this Pale Blue.
Spearmint-comparative is this DecoArt Leprechaun
Orange
Black
White

DIRECTION

Delicately sand the sparkle of the spoons, dust them off and paint them.
Utilize a square of botanical foam to hold them while they dried.
Include white polka dabs up the handles.
Paint earthenware pots white and paint the edges with the hued paint. Include coordinating polka specks.
Cut flower froth into little squares and paste them

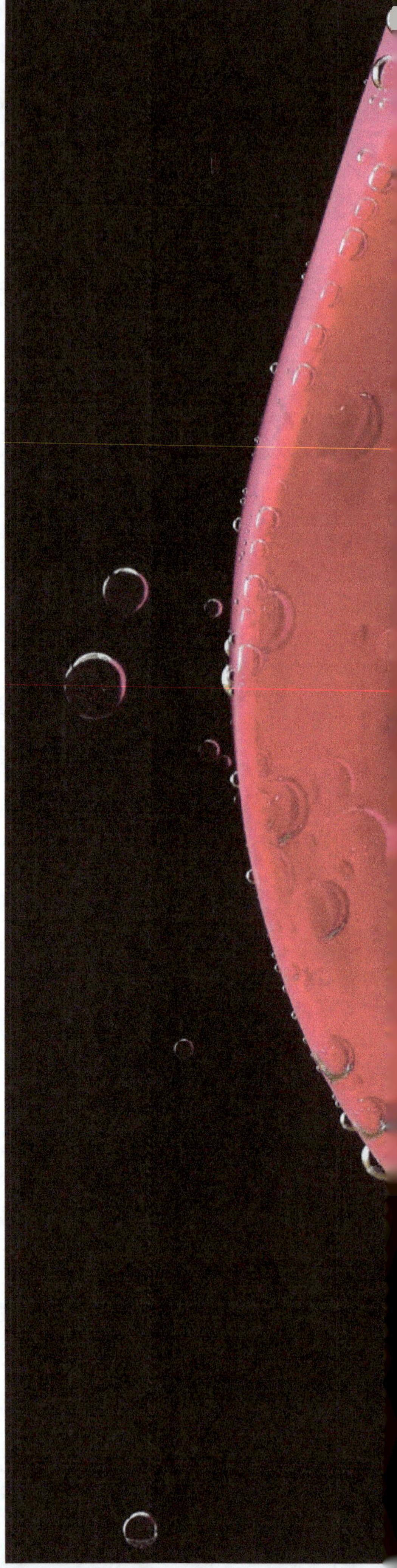

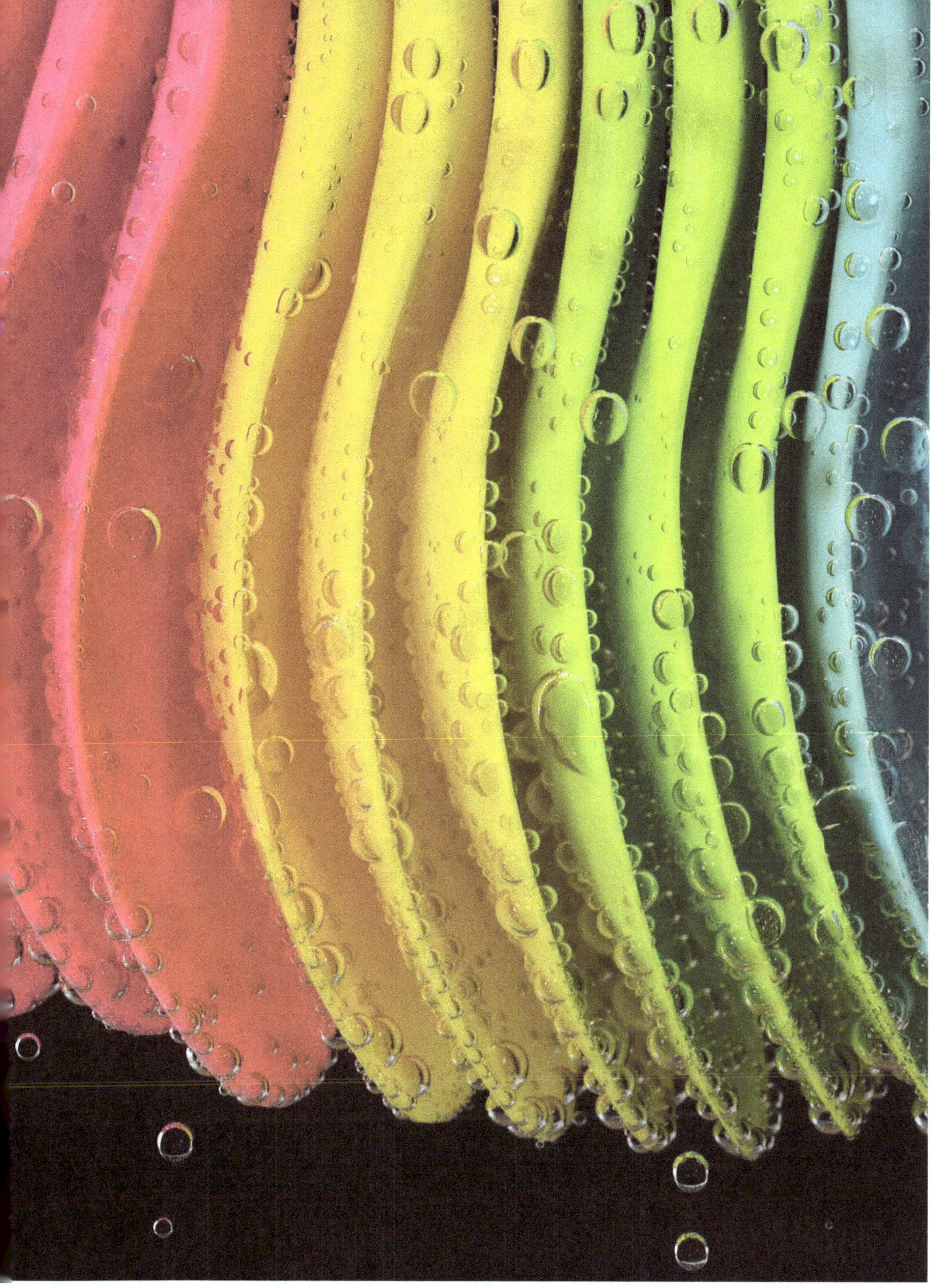

inside the pots. Include the bills and the eyes.
Cut bits of card stock for the informal IDs. Compose names on and include the "hands" utilizing your finger plunged in the paint.
Addition the spoon chicks into the botanical froth. Tie lace into bows and paste to the neck.
Load up with tissue paper and paste on the informal IDs!

REESE WHITE CHOCOLATE EGG WITH SPRINKLES

MATERIALS NEEDED

Hershey's Reese's White Chocolate Eggs
Easter shaded sugar sprinkles.
Small paintbrush
A small bowl of water

DIRECTION

Using your paintbrush, include spots or stripes of water to the outside of the treated egg. You may need to dribble water as the outside of the sweet doesn't hold the water well.
Carefully include sprinkles in the water-painted plan.
Allow the water to dry medium-term. This should bring about the sprinkles solidifying and holding fast to the outside of Reese's Egg.
Carefully pass or brush over any overabundance sprinkles. Utilize a similar paint to get over to delicately apparent abundance.
Tip: If you'd prefer to include various shades of sprinkles, apply one shading and permit it to dry

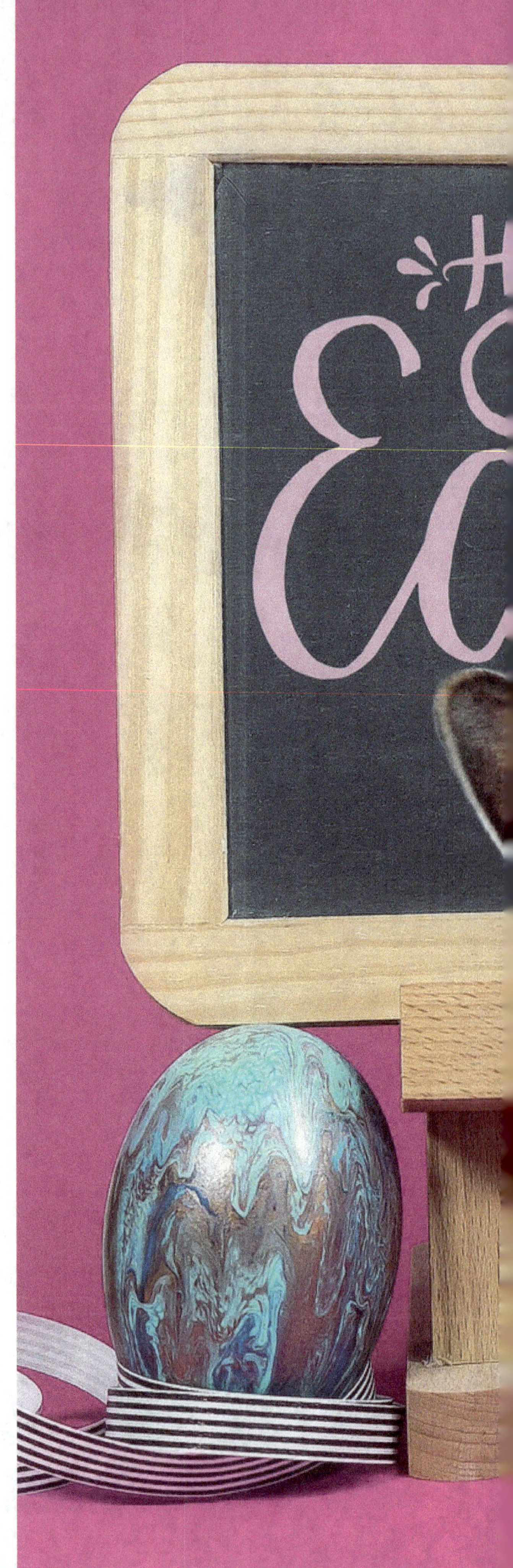

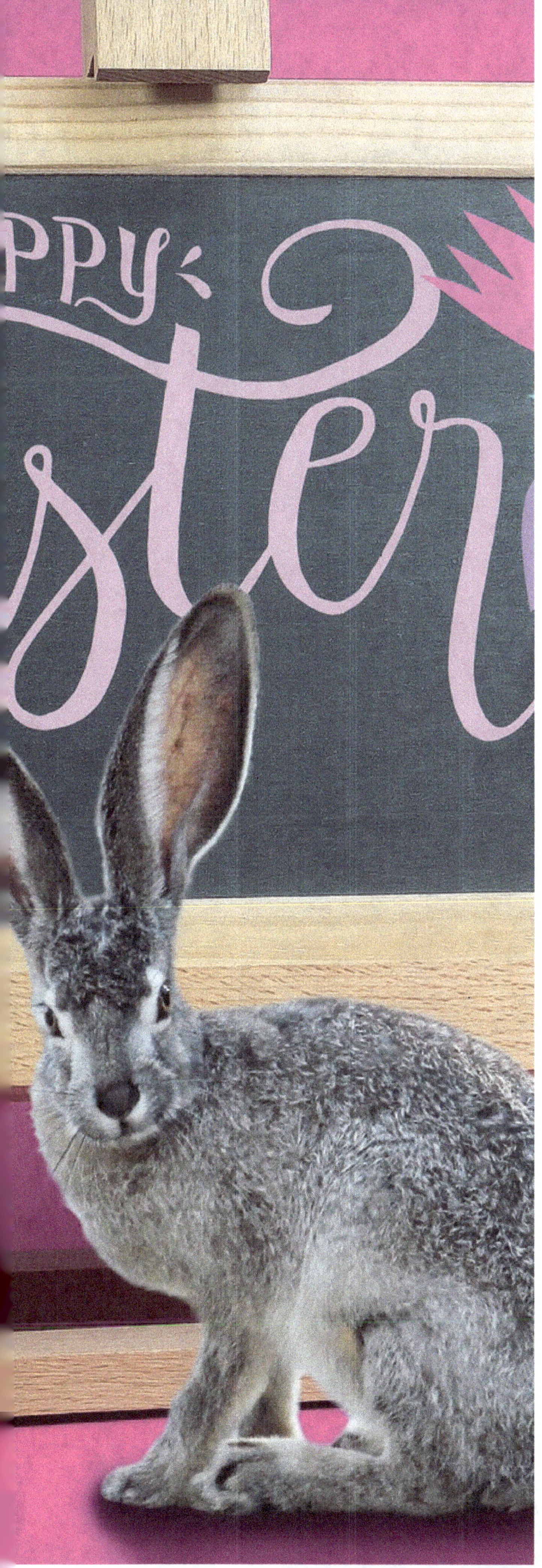

for around 30-an hour and afterward include extra water structures and hues. This will help keep the hues from all seeping into one another.

Paint water on the outside of the treat

CUSTOMIZED EASTER EGG PAILS IN JUST 10 MINUTES

MATERIALS NEEDED

Metal buckets (in the craft paint area of my Jo-Ann Fabric and Craft Stores)

White vinyl, Cricut

Transfer tape, Cricut (it's justified, despite all the trouble!)

Cricut Explore Air (or Cricut Explore with Blue-tooth connector)

Cricut Design Space application for iPad® (or work area variant)

DESIGN: my Hoppy Easter with ears configuration in Design Space

DESIGN: my monogram with eggs and rabbits, handily customized in Design Space

Regular Cricut Mat

DIRECTION

Design - Open my project in Design Space. Tweak it any way you like. Change the hues, cause it longer, to resize it. At that point, send it to your Cricut Explore Air to cut.

Transfer - utilizing move paper, apply the plan to the bucket. It's as easy as putting on a

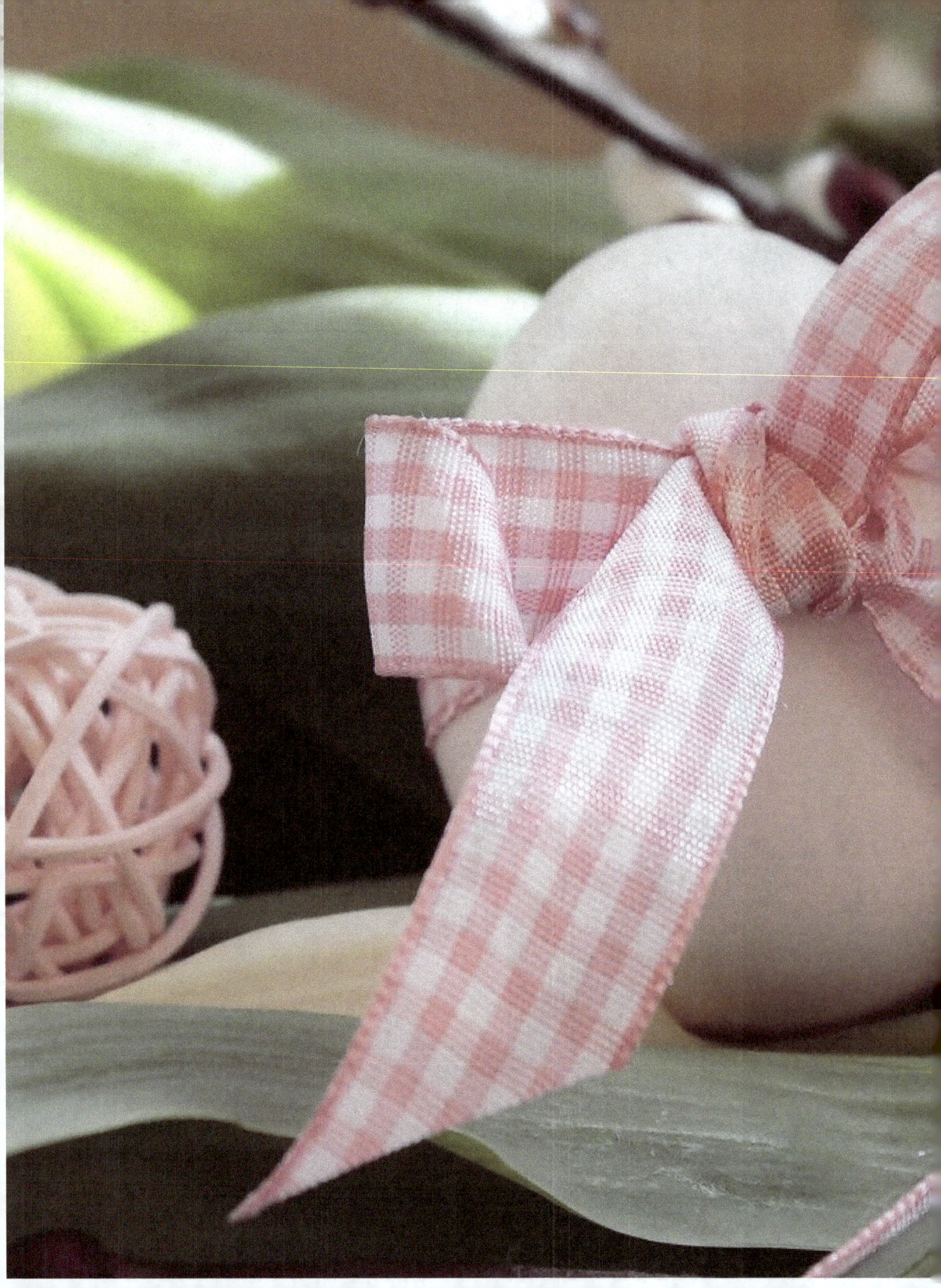

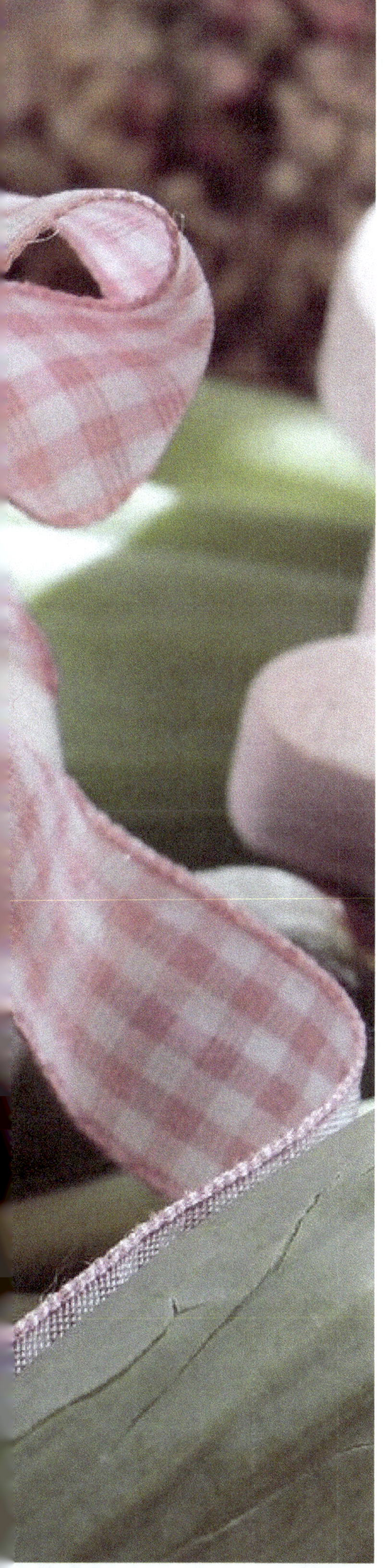

sticker with move tape!
Play - include grass and eggs and play.
It's that easy.

EASTER BRUNCH

MATERIALS NEEDED

Hydrangea, six stem packs
Galvanized blossom container
Green strip
Floral foam, half-circle
Wire cutters
White vinyl
Pink vinyl
Cricut Explore
Cricut light glue tangle
Design Space craftsmanship record

DIRECTION

Cut - cut pack blossoms into single stems
Insert - embed blossom stems into a botanical froth at different statures, trying to fill in all the holes so it looks full
Greenery - in some cases, when you trim blossoms, even counterfeit ones, lose a portion of the leaves. Spare them and fill in any holes, just as haul some out in the front of the course of action
Ribbon - it doesn't generally need to be tied; at times, an excellent wrap works consummately
We should include a DIY monogram. That is to say; we like adding monograms to everything...
Design - in Design Space, alter my structure with

your family beginning and any spring or Easter component that works for your stylistic layout
Cut - place vinyl on the Cricut tangle and cut
Apply - for basic structures (like these), you can apply them by hand, yet for progressively complex plans with bunches of little parts, use Transfer Tape. You'll be happy you did.

EASTER EGG HUNT DYE T-SHIRT

MATERIALS NEEDED

T-shirt (mine originated from Target)
White vinyl
Cricut Explore Air
Cricut cutting mat
Iron
Cricut Design Space - Egg Hunt craftsmanship

DIRECTION

Design - open this Cricut Design Space document. It's estimated for my shirt, yet relying upon the cut of your shirt, you might need to lay your shirt level, measure it over, separate it from locating your middle point, and decide whether you'd like the picture bigger or littler.
Mat - apply the iron on, liner side down, to tangle
Cut - read the bearings on the bundle, yet ensure that you totally "Perfect representation" your cut, or you'll have to glance in a mirror to understand it.
Weed - get rid of all the iron-on that isn't your picture.
Iron - iron your shirt to heat the texture, place the

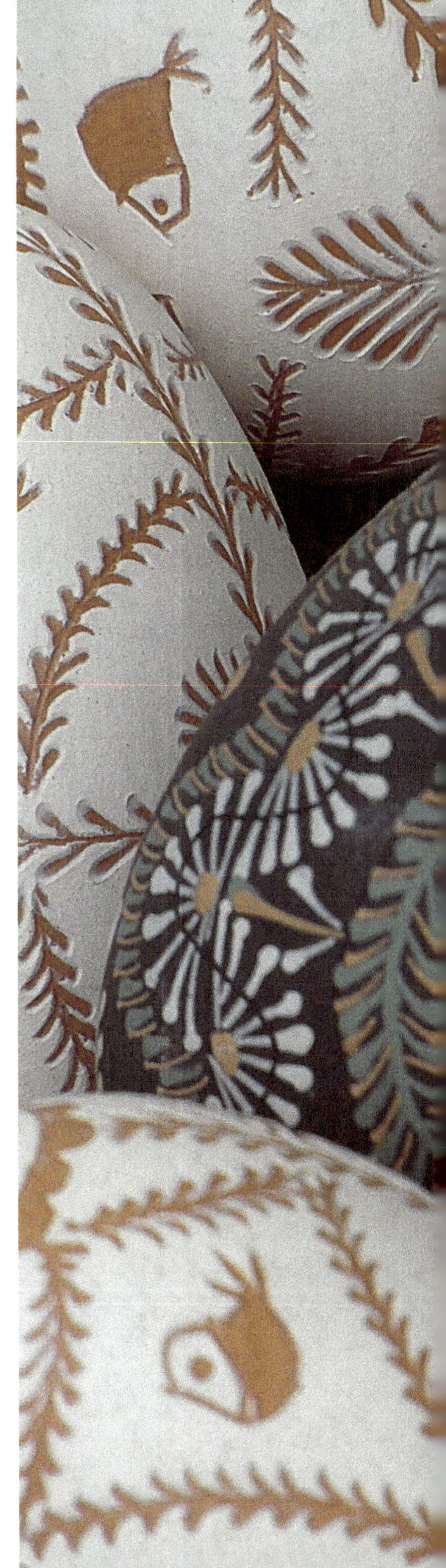

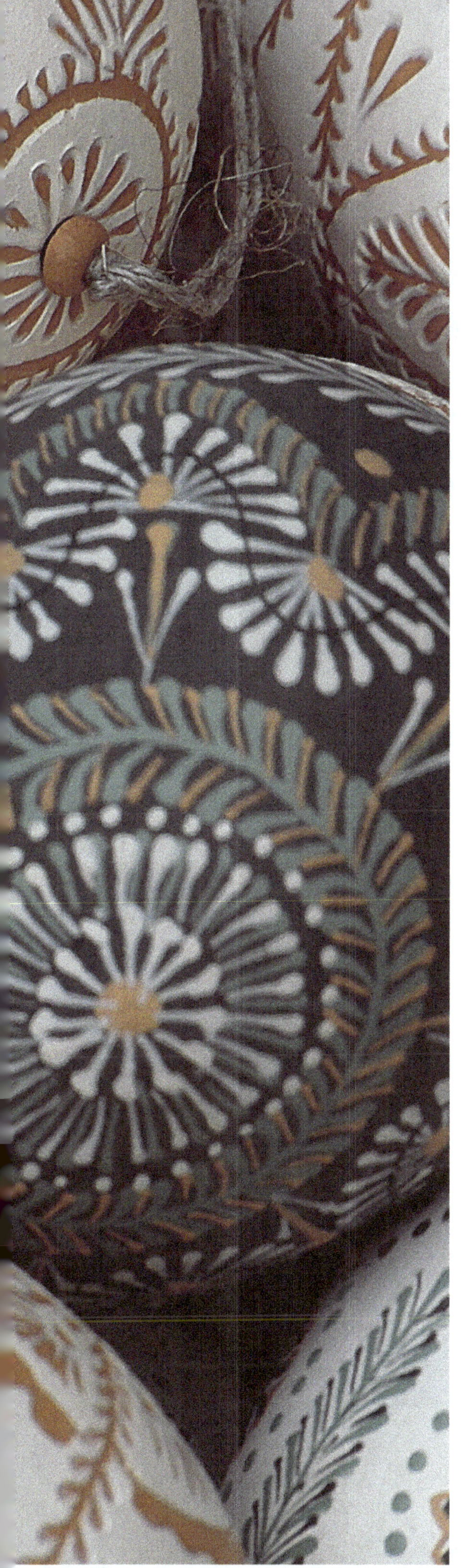

picture with liner on top, iron in 15-second interims. Sparkle takes more heat to apply than ordinary iron-on, so test. Likewise, a smart thought to flip the shirt and iron the back, too, just to even think about making sure it's good to go. Take as much time as is needed!

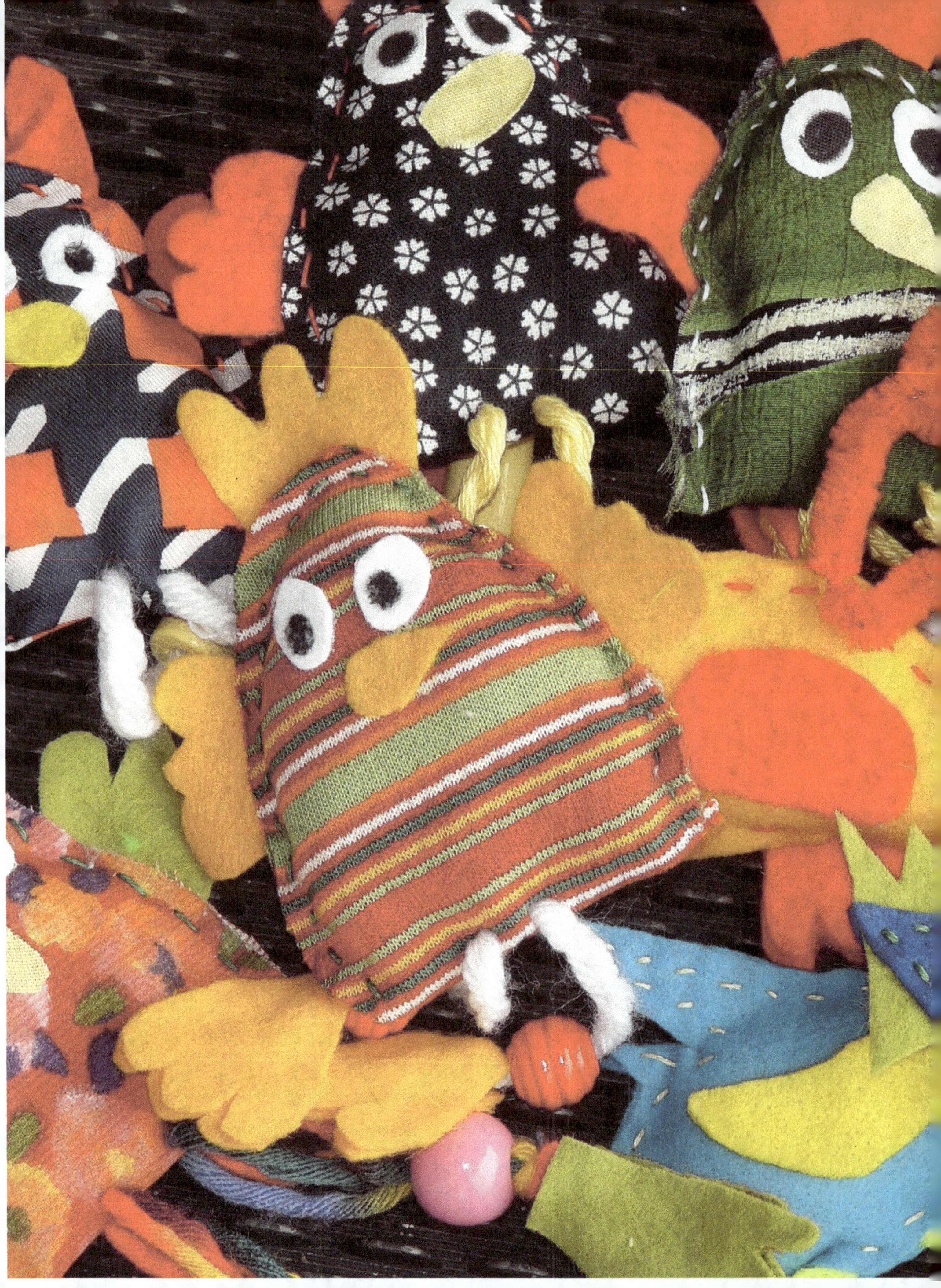

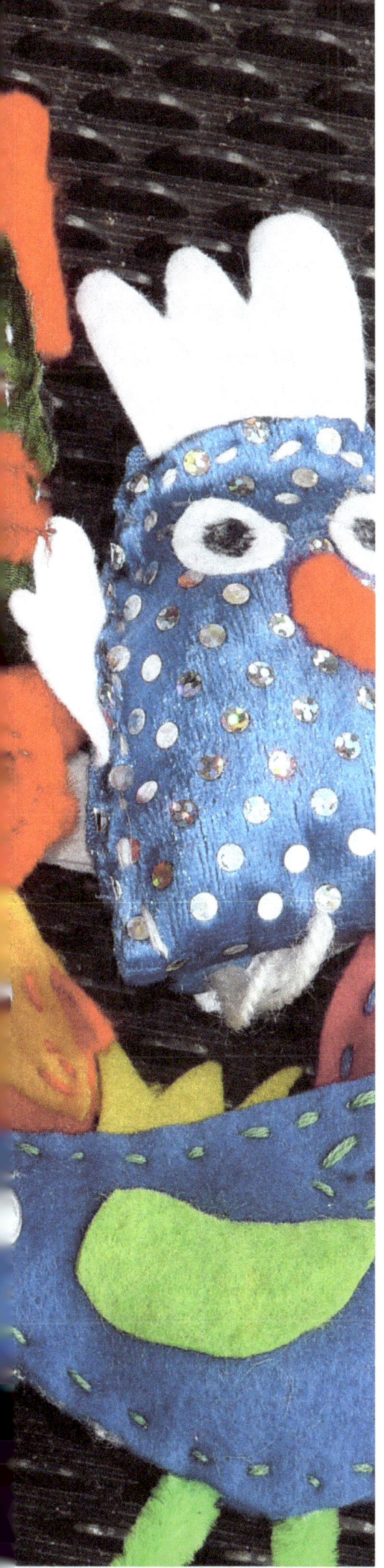

Chapter 7

Other special projects

NO-SEW FELT NATIVITY FINGER PUPPETS

MATERIALS NEEDED

Cricut Producer
Rotary Edge (accompanies Cricut Producer
Cricut Felt Sky Sampler
Cricut Felt Merry go round Sampler
Cricut FabricGrip Tangle
Hot stick weapon and paste sticks

DIRECTION

Open Cricut Configuration Space, and open the record Nativity Finger Manikins
Click Make It and select felt as the material to cut. Load your rotational edge into your machine and load the related shade of felt on the Outline Screen onto your Cricut FabricGrip Tangle.
Once you have removed the majority of your mats, precisely amass every one of the manikins together for a get-together.
Using your heated glue weapon, make a line of paste around the back of the finger manikin. Lay the front piece to finish everything, and press to anchor. At that point, stick the other manikin pieces on, for example, hair, face, and arms. Rehash with every manikin. You will dependably complete

a finger molded line of paste on the back bit of the manikin.

Presently your manikins are finished! Give those little fingers a chance to play away with their Nativity.

DIY SMALLER THAN USUAL CANVAS PENNANTS

MATERIALS NEEDED

Free SVG cut record from Adoration the Day Cricut producer
Light hold tangle
Iron-on Vinyl
EasyPress or iron
Weeding device
Felt
Fabric tangle
Mini canvas standard (we discovered our own at Michaels)
Twine or lace
Dowel bar or thin popsicle stick
Hot paste firearm

DIRECTION

Make a beeline for Adoration the Day, and download the free SVG cut document platitudes that Lindi made. Once you have downloaded the documents, utilize the Cricut to remove your picked saying on press on vinyl. Keep in mind to choose Reflect Cut for this iron-on venture!

Next, weed your adage utilizing the Cricut weeding instrument. Place the idiom on the front of your small-scale canvas pennant.

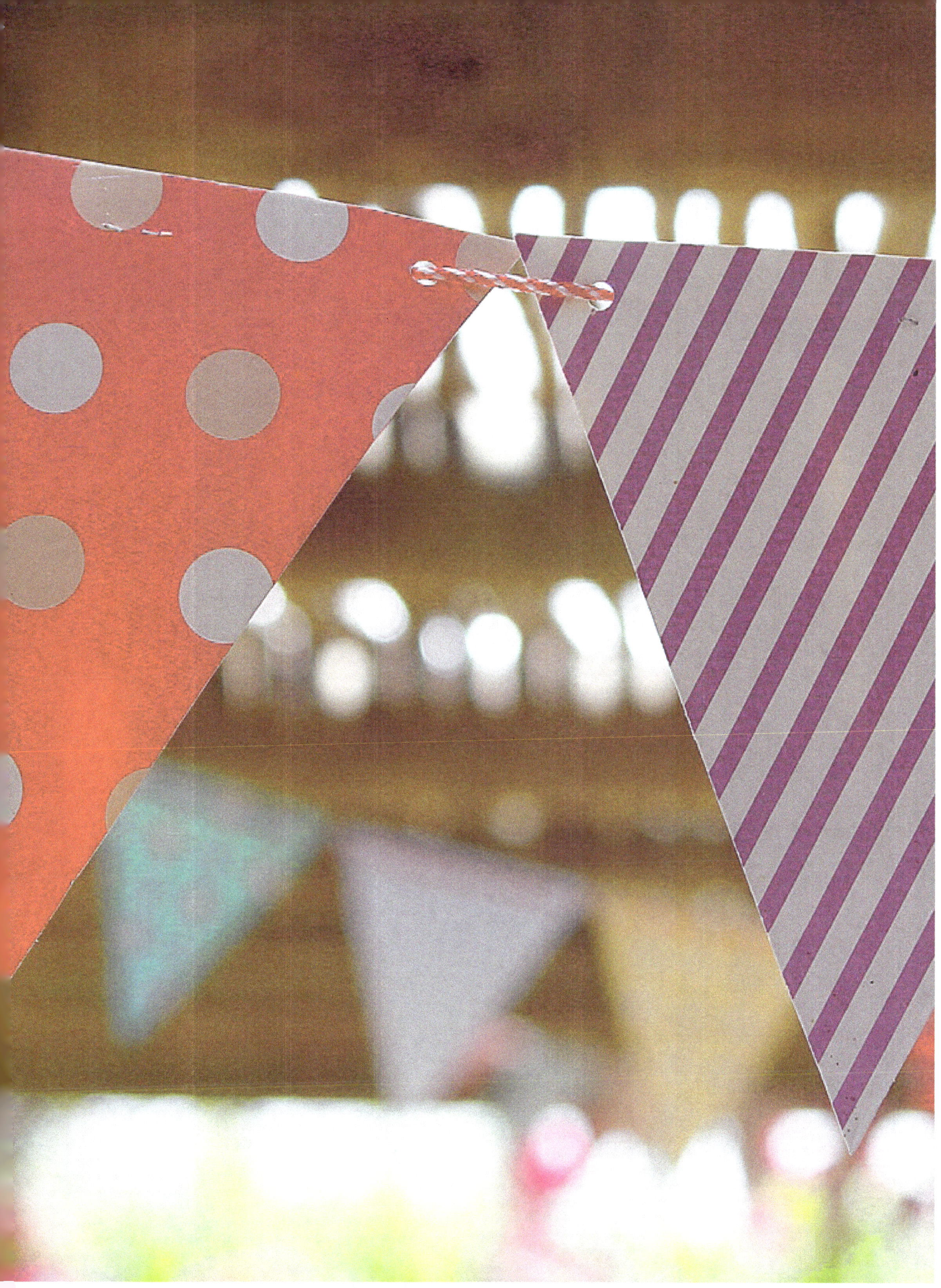

Utilize the new Cricut Simple Press to follow your vinyl saying to the canvas pennant. It accompanies a cheat sheet for temperature settings and a clock to enable you to get the best outcomes in light of the material you are utilizing for your venture.

When you have clung your vinyl to the standard, precisely evacuate the cement backing.

Next comes the fun part. Make a couple of felt blooms in Cricut Configuration Space. I utilized the Bloom Shoppe cartridge to make a wide range of felt blossoms. Likewise, do not hesitate to include any extra embellishments, similar to strip yarn tufts, to your pennant.

Presently it is an excellent opportunity to add the dowel pole to the back of the standard. I made a little pocket for my pole to sneak past and utilized craft glue to anchor it.

Utilize the twine or strip to make the holder for your little standard. Fold the twine over one end of the stick a couple of times and attach the twine to anchor it. Take the rest of the piece and rehash similar strides on the other site.

There you have it, an adorable, snappy, and cheap specialty you can make in under five minutes. I adore how these turned out and had a great time creating with the participants at the Michaels stall at the Cricut Influence Something You To love occasion.

PLANNER STICKERS

MATERIALS NEEDED

Cricut printable sticker paper

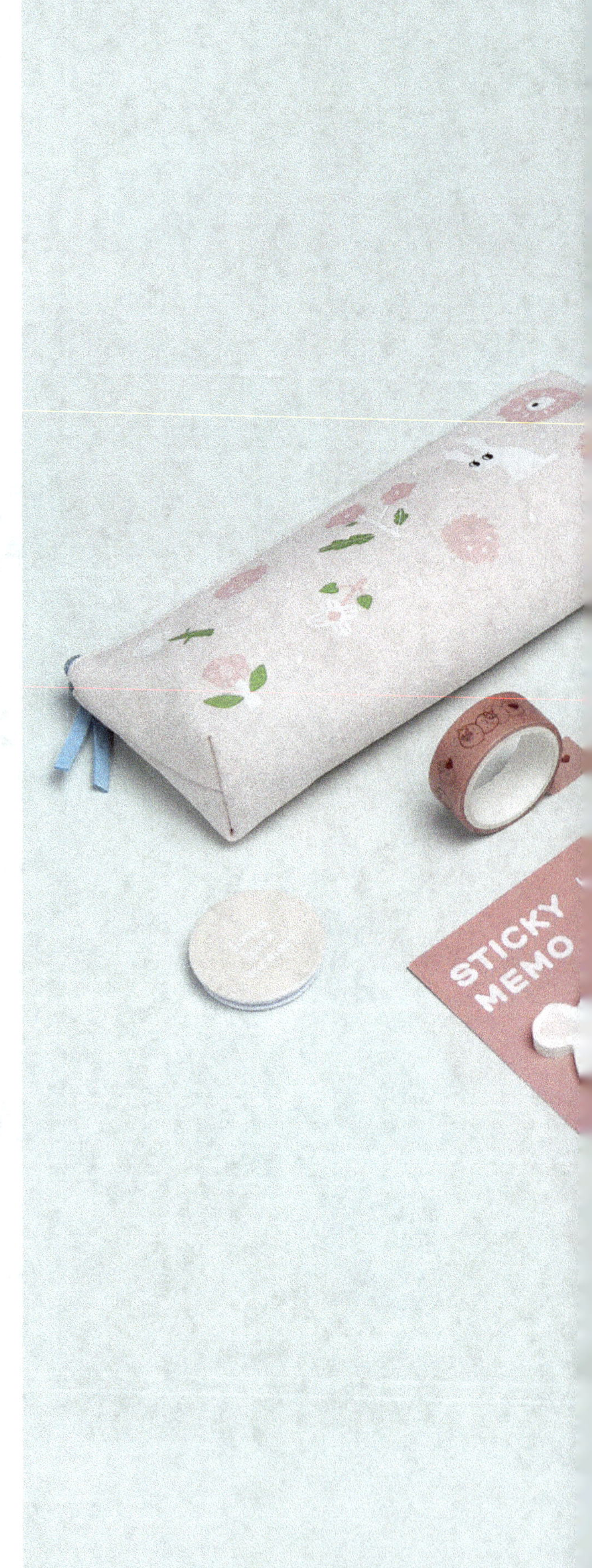

Cricut Explore Air machine or Cricut Maker
Cricut standard cutting mat grip
Printer with ink

DIRECTION

Choose the sticker designs. You can choose from the Design shop or upload your own. Start by opening the Design Space program and click on the Image option. Then, head to the search function and locate the planner stickers. Locate which one you want to use. Place the choices on the canvas and arrange them in the order that you would like them to be.

Click the Make It option. Design Space will direct you to begin printing the image. Follow the directions to print the images.

To proceed, place the stickers in the Cricut to cut the stickers out.

WOODLAND FOX BOOKMARK

MATERIALS NEEDED

Cricut weeding tool
Multiple colors of cardstock
Adhesive
Standard cutting mat grip
Cricut machine

DIRECTION

Open your Design shop, and use the design

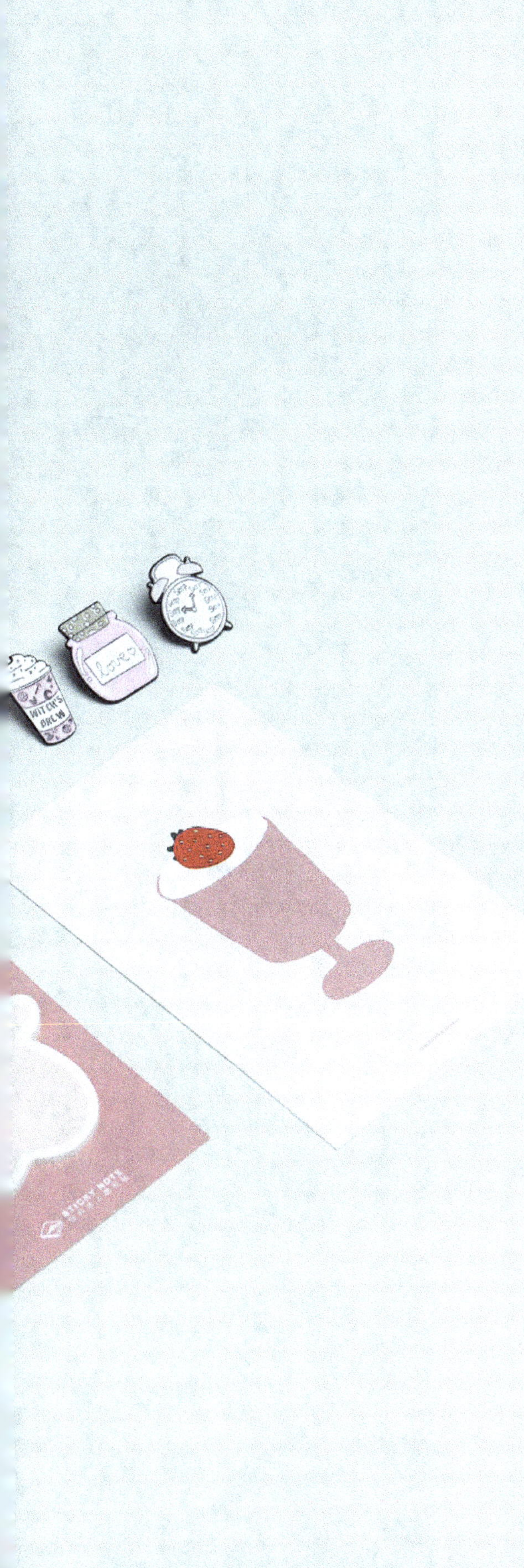

file that you have created for this bookmark.

You may have to purchase the file that is needed to design this bookmark.

Cut two pieces for the bookmark. One for each side of the bookmark. This helps it to be sturdier.

You will need to glue the two identical pieces together.

Once you send the image to the Cricut machine, you can begin to place your paper's color on the mat. Then, cut it out. Continue to do this until all the pieces and colors have been cut.

Weed out any unnecessary pieces that come out with the fox.

Glue the fox together, and then glue it to the bookmark backing. You do not want to use too much glue. This will keep the cardstock from being soggy. Use a heavy book and place the bookmark between the pages to get the glue to set and the bookmark not to wave.

DIY MERMAID BIRTHDAY CARD

MATERIALS NEEDED

White cardstock
Cricut Explore Air machine
Light cutting mat grip
0.mm Cricut pen

DIRECTION

Open your Design shop file and chose the Image option. If you have Cricut Access, you should be able to use the mermaid image for free; if not, it

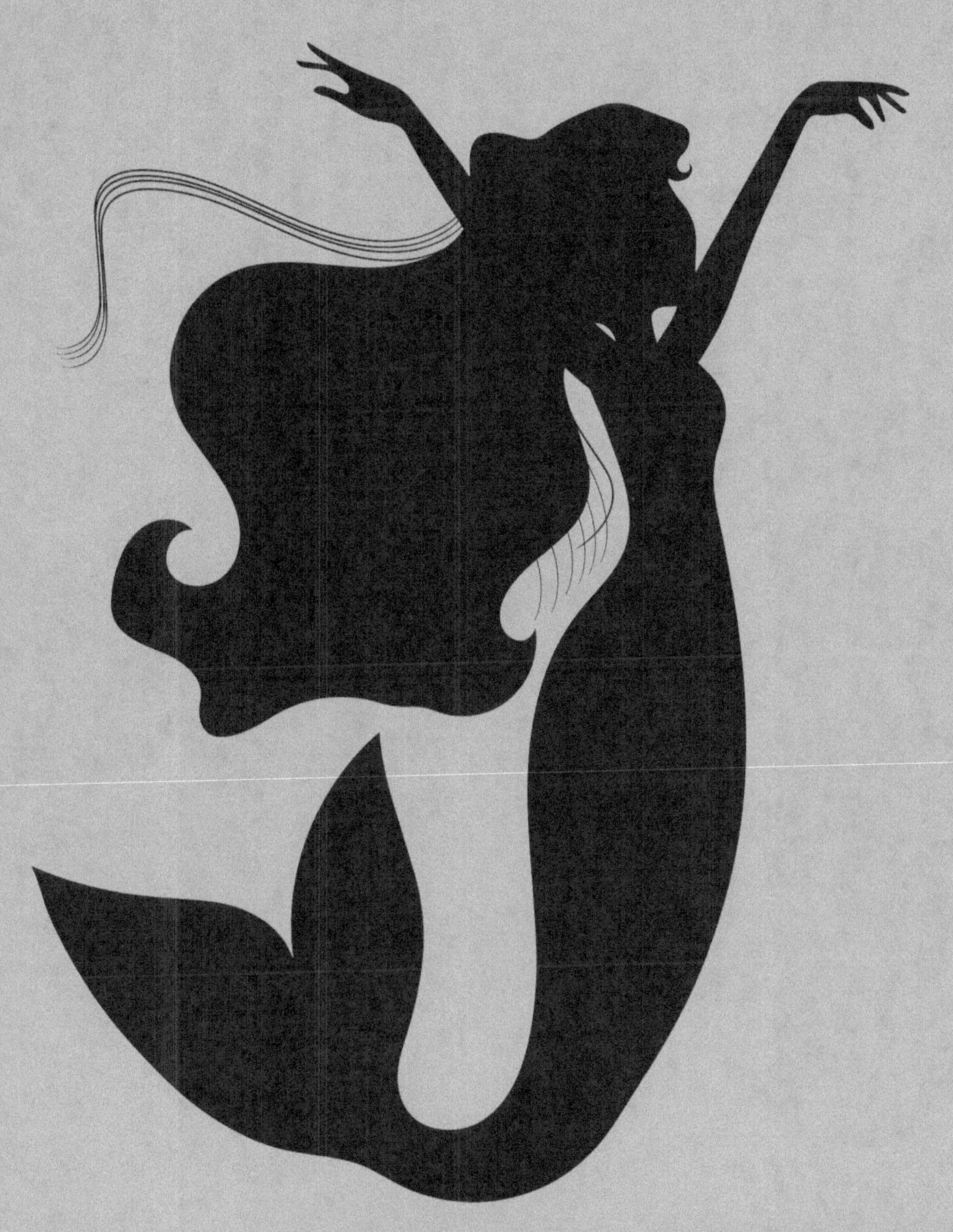

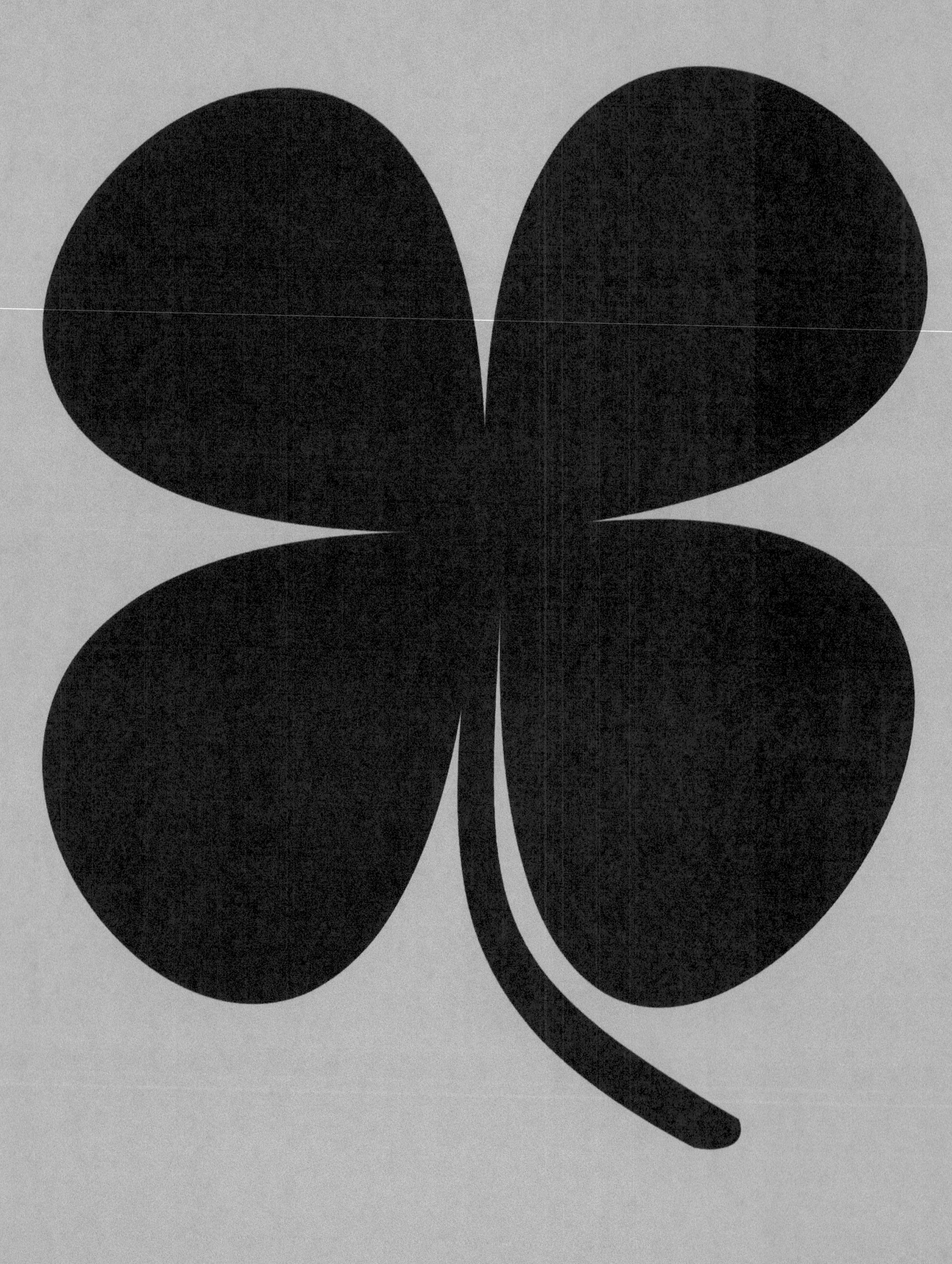

will cost you some money.

Use your white stock by placing it on the cutting mat and insert it into the machine. Set the dial to Cardstock. Insert your pen set to black into the pen holder of the cartridge.

Send your project to the Design Space, and wait patiently to process and draw the image.

When the card is done, present it to the expected birthday girl.

SHAMROCK EARRINGS

MATERIALS NEEDED:

Cricut Maker
Earring (from a Cricut Project)
Rotary Wheel
Knife Blade
FabricGrip Mat
StrongGrip Mat
Weeder Tool
Cricut Leather
Scraper Tool
Adhesive
Pebbled-Faux Leather
Earring Hooks

DIRECTION

First, open the Cricut Project (Earring). You can now either click on 'Make It' or 'Customize' to edit it. Once you have selected one, click on 'Continue'. The cut page immediately pops up, selects your material, and waits for the 'Load' tools and Mat to appear.

Make your Knife blade your cutting tool in clamp B. This will be used on the Leather.

On the StrongGrip Mat, place the Leather and make sure it is facing down. Then load the Mat into the machine and tap the 'Cut' flashing button.

When the scoring has been done, go back to the cutting tool and change it to Rotary Wheel so that you can use it on the Faux Leather.

Similarly, place your Faux leather on your FabricGrip Mat, facing down. Then load the Mat into the machine and tap the 'Cut' flashing button.

Take away all the items on the Mat with your Scraper tool. Be careful with the small fringes, though.

Make a hole on the top circle by making use of the Weeder tool. Make sure the hole is large enough to make the Earring hooks fit in.

If necessary, you may have to twist the hook's end with the pliers to fit them in.

Close them up after you have looped them inside the hole that was made inside the Earring.

Finally, you should glue the Shamrock to the surface of the Earring with adhesive.

Wait for it to dry before using.

WALL DECALS

MATERIALS NEEDED

Adhesive vinyl
Cricut machine
Weeding tool
Scrapper tool

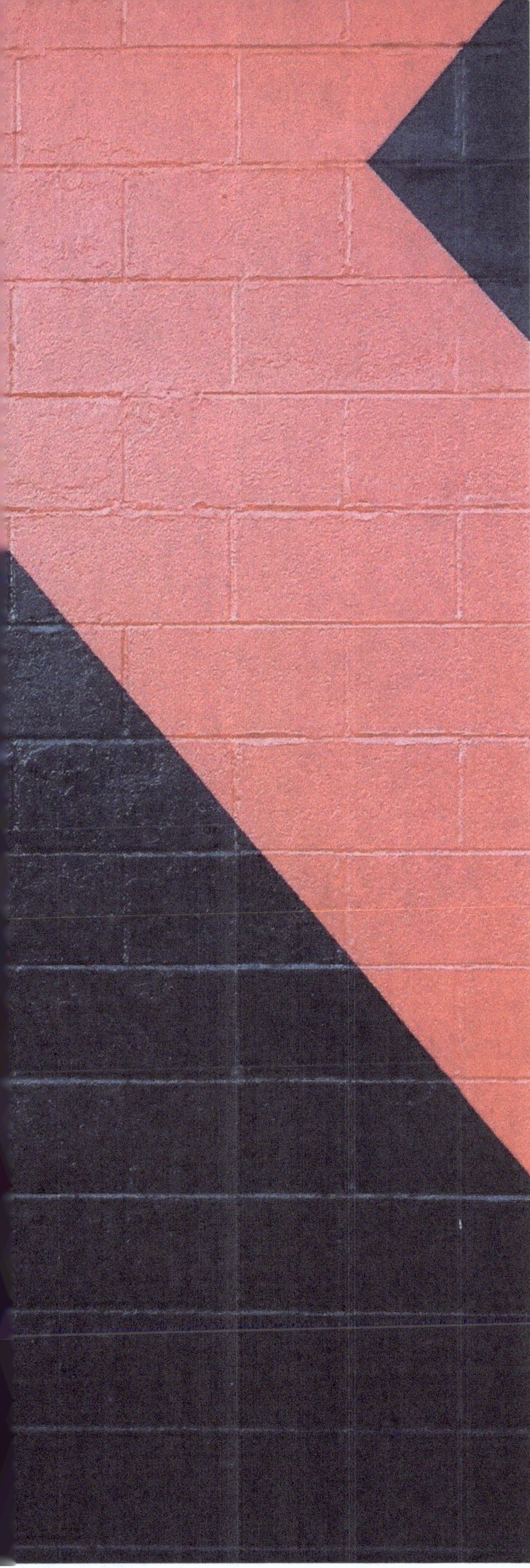

DIRECTION

Log in to the Cricut design space.
Create a 'New Project'.
Click on 'Upload Image'.
Drag the image to the design space.
Highlight the image and 'Flatten' it.
Click on the 'Make It' button.
Place vinyl on the cutting mat.
Custom dial the machine to vinyl.
Load the cutting mat into the machine.
Push the mat up against the rollers.
Cut the design out of the vinyl.
Weed out the excess vinyl with a weeding tool.
Apply a thin layer of transfer tape on the vinyl.
Peel off the backing.
Apply the transfer tape on the wall.
Smoothen with a scraper tool to let out the air bubble.

PERSONALIZED PILLOWS

MATERIALS NEEDED

Black, dark blue, or dark purple fabric
Heat transfer vinyl in gold or silver
Cutting mat
Polyester batting
Weeding tool or pick
Cricut EasyPress

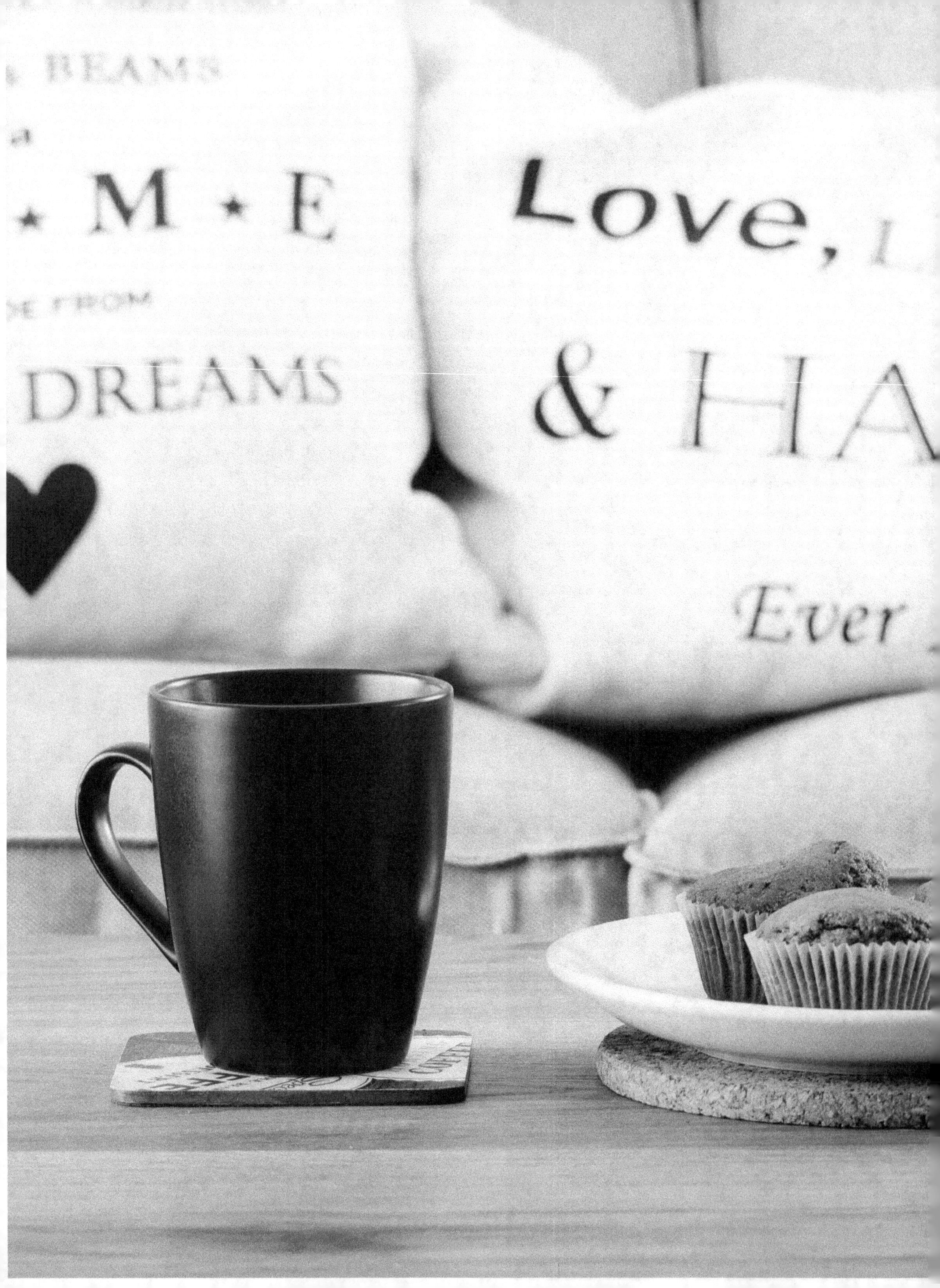

& BEAMS
a
* M * E
E FROM
DREAMS
Love, L
& HA
Ever

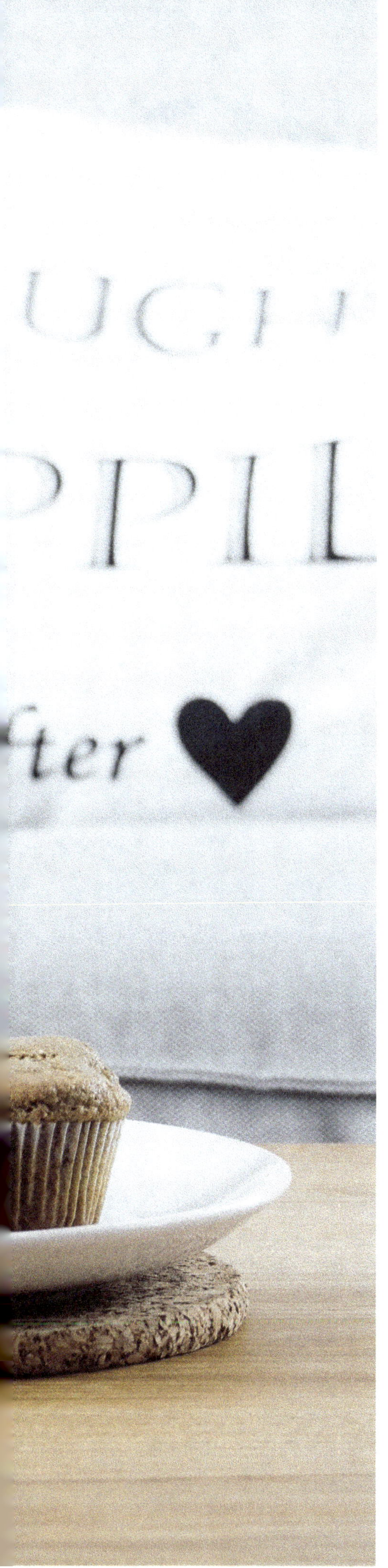

DIRECTION

Decide the shape you want for your pillow, and cut two matching shapes out of the fabric.
Open Cricut Design Space, and create a 'New Project'.
Select the 'Image' button in the lower left-hand corner and search 'Stars'.
Select the stars of your choice and click 'Insert'.
Place the iron-on material on the mat.
Send the design to the Cricut.
Use the weeding tool, or pick to remove excess material.
Remove the material from the mat.
Place the iron-on material on the fabric.
Use the EasyPress to adhere it to the iron-on material.
Sew the two fabric pieces together, leaving allowance for a seam and a small space open.
Fill the pillow with polyester batting through the small open space.
Sew the pillow shut.
Cuddle up to your starry pillow

Chapter 8
Tips for making money and setting crafting business

THINGS TO CONSIDER BEFORE STARTING YOUR CRAFT BUSINESS

To start with, you may want to track your income and expenses on a spreadsheet. But when possible, invest in software such as Quicken. This will make your job much more comfortable. Plus, you can print out reports to take to your accountant once a year. This will decrease his fees since he'll have less work to do.

Starting a sideline business can be time-consuming. It's best if you can get your family on board from the beginning. Let them know how the extra money will stress the family budget or maybe help pay for an unforgettable vacation. If your family knows what you're working towards, they'll be more excited about helping you. Teenagers may be able to work in the business with you and learn valuable skills.

HOW TO PRICE YOUR PRODUCTS

When deciding how to price your products, consider the following costs:

Price of material Your time Business expenses for advertising and website hosting time you spend marketing your business Packing materials Shipping

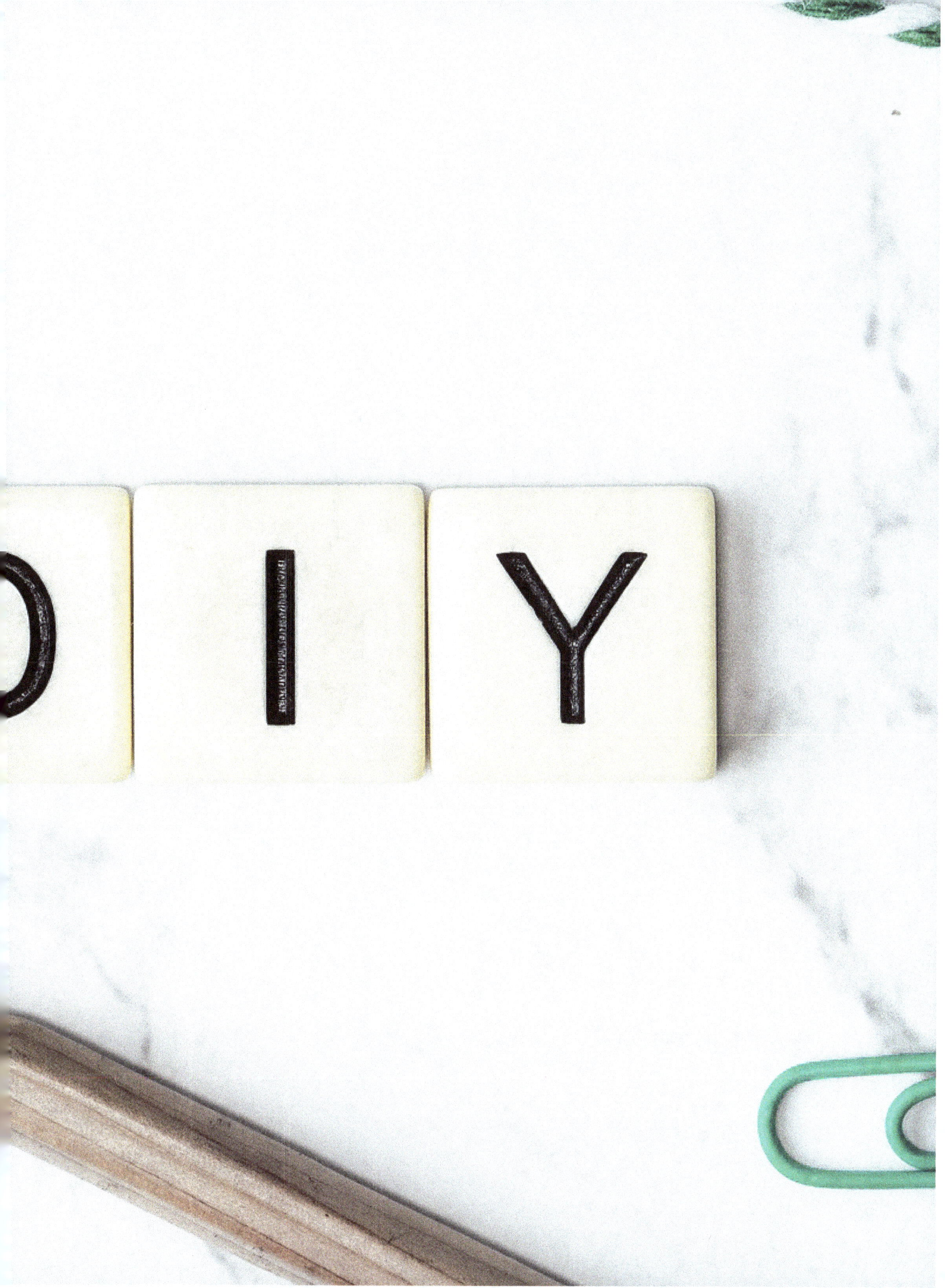
DIY

costs

Many crafters devalue their time. Decide how much you want to make per hour. Then determine how much time each project takes you to complete. Add your time into the equation. Otherwise, you'll burn out fast and won't make much of a profit.

When marketing your crafts, always be aware of upcoming holidays. Mark your calendar so your projects are ready in plenty of time for holiday shoppers. You may think that after Christmas, all online shopping ceases for a while. But January is usually the second busiest month of the year. So, take advantage of the shopping mentality and get your items in front of hungry buyers.

REMEMBER TO CREATE PROJECTS FOR A PERSONAL HOLIDAY SUCH AS

Anniversaries Baby births Graduations Housewarming New Job Promotions Retirement Weddings. People are always celebrating something. Create projects based on special occasions.

Offering personalization can be a huge marketing advantage and can apply to any item like wine glasses, decorative wall hangings, or sports teams. These items are considered of more excellent value if they've been custom ordered and made specifically for the buyer using their initials or child's name.

ATTEMPT TO BE DIVERSE

Indeed be unique. Carry to the plate your theatricality and imagination.

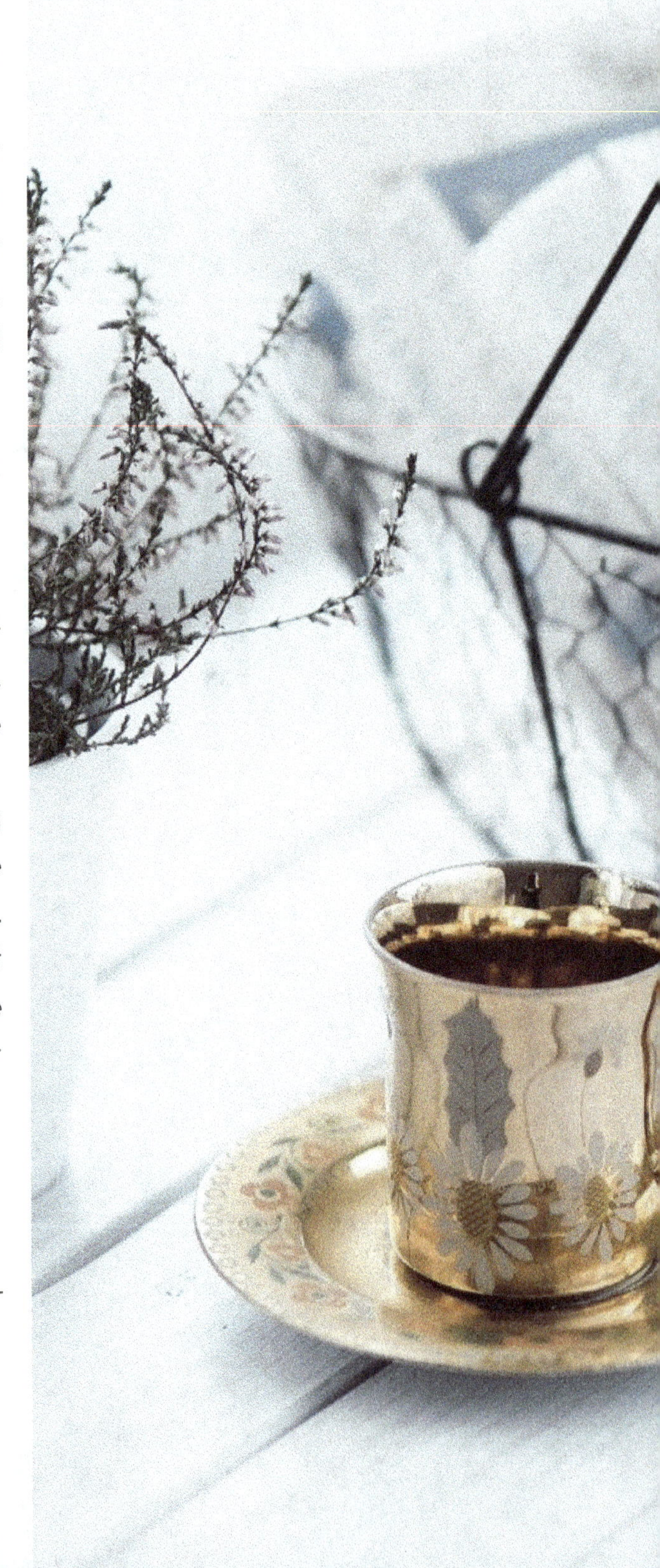

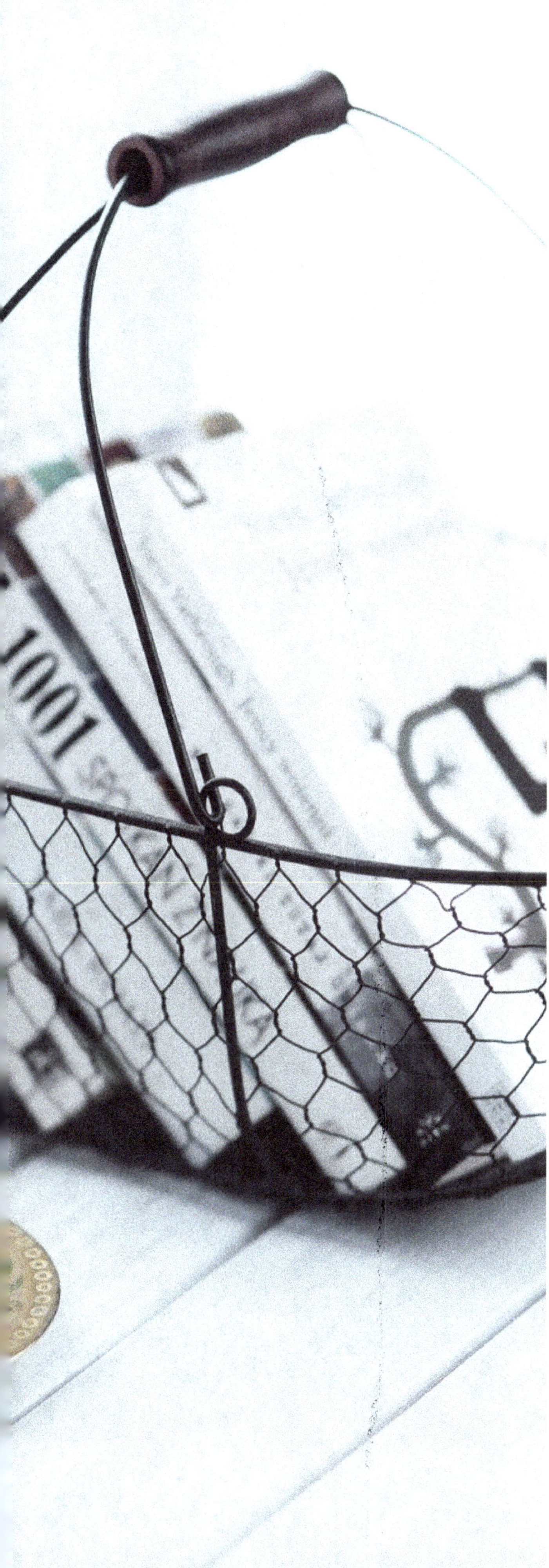

I'm sure you'd agree with the standout title tiles if you've been in Cricut's designs for any time duration. They became a mad success, and then they were all marketing them.

In the crafting universe, that's how it works, isn't it? But you may be one of the first individuals to get on a wave pattern trip once the next hot sale comes along. And if you're not patient, the process of handling Cricut crafts may get tiresome and pricey.

Bear in mind that I'm not asking you to innovate the chair, just to introduce a theme and flourish to your own.

And when the craft appears like someone else's, the truth is, it's only going to become a trade battle. Nobody's winning.

So when someone else is zigging, you zag. Had this one?

CONTINUE REFINING IT

You will think that producing and selling something under the sun would give you more choice, hence more clients, hence more income. That's not the way it operates, though. More prices, more exhaustion, and more non-selling goods are what it would offer you. Do not aspire to be the design world's Walmart; strive to be a professional, and the greatest of your region of inventiveness is available. So take a moment to determine what you are going to be remembered for.

BE IMMUNE

Work regularly on your Cricut design project. Ideally, each day you can be focusing on it. Any of you might only choose to offer it as a passion and might only be willing to work once a week on it.

Do so as frequently as you can, whatever the routine is. If you neglect your company for days or weeks on end, you're hardly going to get far. Be compliant with prices and also with consistency. Your clients need to know what to demand from you. If they feel they can rely on you, they can suggest you to everyone else again and again.

HOW MANY DO YOU WANT?

You'll be well able to market the goods for sale until you have the expense of materials. If you enjoy working for minimum wage, don't overlook the time it would take you to build the piece.

A good rule of thumb is that the purchase price would be two and four times the production rate. Don't fear because people are giggling at you that it's too much. You're the initial, you've narrowed the scope down, and you're a professional, and you're the greatest at what you're doing. And (more on that quickly) you are utilizing premium goods. People would pay for it happily. Paying for crafts cash.

LEARN FRESH DAILY ANYTHING

Do not be ashamed of knowing about others before you have left. You don't have to find out all by yourself.

Everyone has already done it if you want to learn how to ascend the Etsy ranks or build a good Facebook community, and now they share all the tips and tricks
they know.

At least you'll be doing more selling than crafts at the start of your Cricut Company, making it a priority to discover something fresh that applies to your company every day.

TIPS FOR SELLING CRICUT PROJECTS ON ETSY

ESTABLISH YOUR BRAND

Etsy is so popular that they pride themselves in bringing artists and customers together to develop a relationship. So, it's your job to tell people who you are and why they should buy from you.

To build your credibility, post videos on YouTube that explain the process you use to create crafts. This helps brand you as an expert. Plus, even though viewers might like to learn to do the projects themselves, they often decide it's not worth the time and effort and will click through to purchase from your website. Always link back to your main website or craft store from your social media sites. Set up your signature to include your business contact information when posting to online forums and in your email.

Keep your business name in front of your customers and make it easy for them to find you. Include a business card or refrigerator magnet with your company info on it with every new order. Include an extra business card and ask them to hand it to a friend.

THE CUSTOMER IS ALWAYS RIGHT.

Always offer excellent customer service. If someone emails you with a question, get back to them as soon as possible. Package and ship your products carefully. Make sure you add enough to your shipping costs to allow for postage and packaging. You may want to offer gift wrapping for an extra charge.

Ask for feedback. It's the best way to find out how to improve your service. Make it easy for customers to leave testimonials on your web page. A happy customer goes a long way in building your credibility. State your return or refund policy clearly on your website, so there are no surprises for your customers.

Creating projects with your Circuit can be more than just a fun hobby. If you're willing to put in the effort, you can build a sideline or even a full-time business while doing something you love.

REGULATION OF CONSISTENCY

Market-priced merchandise. Any day of the week, consistency dominates over quantities. Let's have a peek at these two custom baskets below for Easter.

The buckets are possibly overlooked or trashed because they were poorly made and inexpensive to purchase. Easter comes and goes.

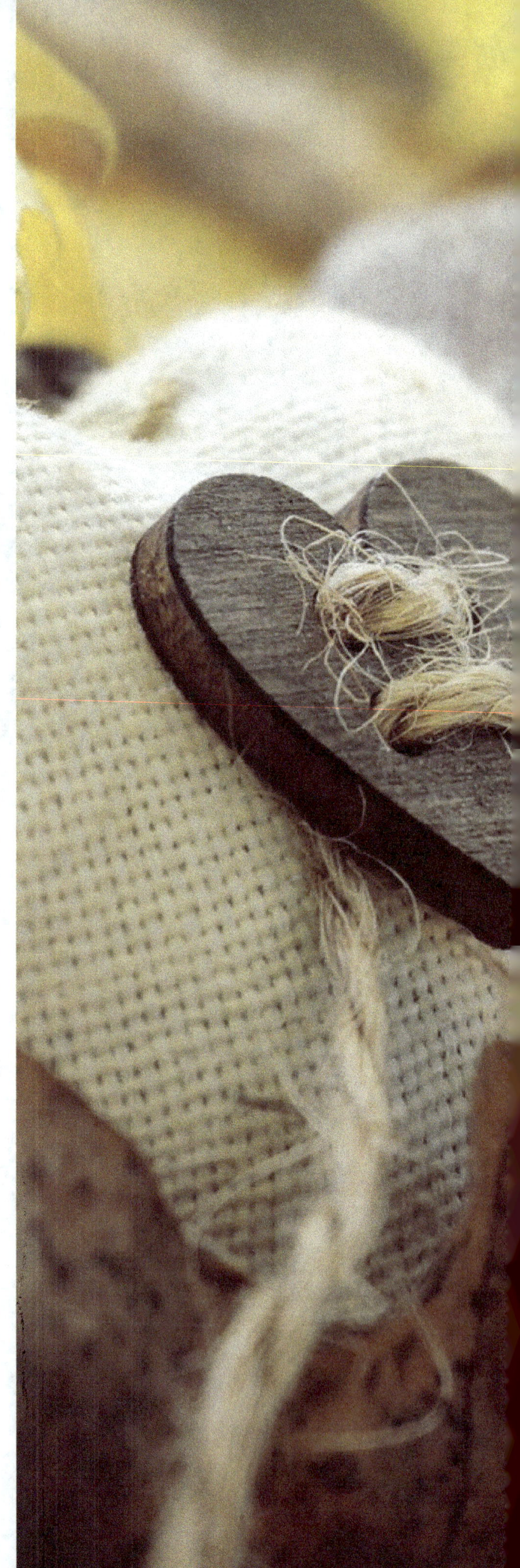

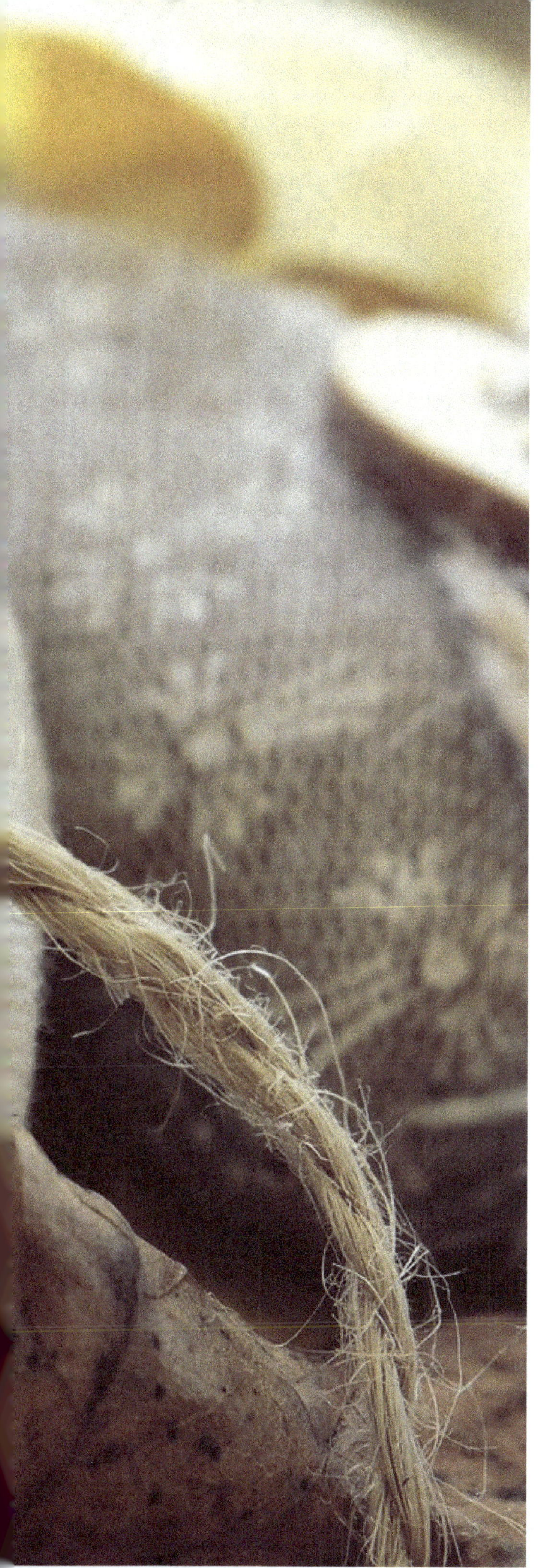

Easter buckets on the left now. They are cotton, and they are accurate of higher quality. They stick out, and if other crafters are selling them, not all are. You are studying each day, and you realize that these bundles will be used long beyond Easter if we only placed the label on them, and we sell them as such. For the empty basket, we charged $8.00 and for the heat transfer vinyl, $1.00, with a combined cost of $9.00. We market them for $25.00, which makes us $16.00 in profit for each one that we offer.

Within a second, let that sink. Less job ensures more personal time or enjoyable or learning time.

People will pay for service, and for service, they will suggest you to their mates. The most

Introduction

First of all, thank you for purchasing my guide: "Cricut Joy Complete Collection" . I'm Sienna Tally, and in this guide, the long-awaited follow-up to "Cricut Joy Vol 1" and "Cricut Joy vol. 2 ", I will take you on a journey of discovery into the colorful world of Cricut projects. Specifically, we will learn what types of objects the latest Cricut model can create, but most importantly, how to make fantastic creations for you and your family.

The Cricut is an incredible machine for individuals into adoration making and for or individuals who need to cut many things with various kinds of materials. A Cricut is a cutting machine, and fantasy worked out as expected for some crafters. Below are some advantages of having a Cricut machine.

Something that sets the Cricut Maker separated from other cutting machines is that it has a few exchangeable edges. Need to do some sewing, sewing, paper, create foam, balsa wood, felt, foil, burlap, cardstock, grain box, creased cardboard, basic food item sack, or a bazillion (alright, slight embellishment) different undertakings? This machine can deal with it to such an extent!

Set your eyes on the bigger goals. Once you have the expense of provisions, you'll be more ready to value your things to sell. Remember the time it took you to make the thing except if you like working for nothing. A dependable general guideline is your selling cost will be between two to multiple times your expense of provisions. Try not to stress over individuals snickering at you that it's excessive. You're unique, you've limited your field, and you're a specialist and the best at what you do. Besides, you're utilizing quality items (more on that soon).

Gain some new useful knowledge every day. Don't fear gaining from the individuals who have gone before you. You don't need to make sense of everything all alone. In any event, toward the beginning of your Cricut business, you'll be accomplishing more advertising than making. Make it an objective This Here is Sienna Tally writing to you! Given the breadth of projects I'd like to offer you the adventure doesn't end here! In fact, I'll be back soon with another guide dedicated to materials and individual occasions. It's time to get crafting! Enjoy your new knowledge of your fantastic machine and give a new project a try. The beauty of the Cricut is the versatility of functions and user-friendly format. Use this to make your life and home and those of your friends and family more exciting and beautiful!

Now that you have completed this handy manual on using the Cricut machine, you should be well-equipped to head out into the Cricut crafting world and start designing your favorite crafts today. With each single Cricut cartridge, you can set up a specific image or design that you can reuse every day. There are a few limitations, but mostly it is how high your imagination can go.

So, make that card, cut those felt flowers, a design that excellent quotable sign, or create some lovely new earrings for you or your best friend to wear. Whatever it is that you want to create, the Cricut has gotten you covered with the machine's versatility. If you need a portable one, you are in luck since the Cricut Mini is designed to go with you anywhere you have internet and a computer.

As you gain more experience using the computer and try new features, you can solve almost all of them.

The next step is to find projects and materials that excite you and dive right in! It would be great to see you embrace the vast number of crafting opportunities that now lie ahead of you.

Tweak the ideas in this book to fit you perfectly. Change up the materials, the blanks, what the design is, and whatever else your imagination can come up with. Create your projects, as well. Following the ideas in this book will give you a good foundation for using your Cricut. Once you've become familiar with it in the different ways you can use it, you can let your creativity flow and create whatever you want.

HAPPY CRAFTING

Thank you !!